Discover Creativity with Babies

This book explores creative development in babies and shows how practitioners can support even the youngest child's natural curiosity and help them to develop their ideas, thoughts and feelings. It provides engaging, cost-effective and achievable activity ideas to support the developing creative mind, covering the outdoors; communication and language; and personal, social, emotional and physical development.

Including discussion boxes, case studies and reflective points in every chapter, Day offers guidance and insight into key topics and well-known theories, including

- how and why to facilitate creativity,

- adult–baby relationships and attachment,

- the environment and resources that enable creativity and

- outdoor exploration and play.

Discover Creativity with Babies is a wonderful guide for early years practitioners looking to support and cultivate the curious and creative side to every child, however they may choose to express it.

Louise Day is Manager of Wally's Day Nursery, UK.

Discover Creativity with Babies

Louise Day

Routledge
Taylor & Francis Group

LONDON AND NEW YORK

First edition published 2021
by Routledge
2 Park Square, Milton Park, Abingdon, Oxon, OX14 4RN

and by Routledge
52 Vanderbilt Avenue, New York, NY 10017

Routledge is an imprint of the Taylor & Francis Group, an informa business

British Library Cataloguing-in-Publication Data
A catalogue record for this book is available from the British Library

Library of Congress Cataloging-in-Publication Data
A catalog record has been requested for this book

ISBN: 978-0-367-36783-1 (hbk)
ISBN: 978-0-367-36786-2 (pbk)
ISBN: 978-0-429-35147-1 (ebk)

Typeset in Bembo
by KnowledgeWorks Global Ltd.

Contents

About the Author

Discover Creativity…is a series of books that will explore the development of creativity in young children from birth to five years. It will explore some of the definitions of creativity and why it matters to children in their early years whilst looking at the relationships that matter the most to young children and how we can foster creative thinking in our settings to ensure that we give our children the best possible start. It will look at the environments that are conducive to creativity and the vital role of the adult in the process. Each book contains information relating to children of the given age as well as inspiration for those working closely with them to support and encourage a generation of creative thinkers.

The first book in the series, *Discover Creativity…Babies*, looks specifically at babies up to the age of two. It explores their early milestones, crucial attachments and the development of creativity and how this can be fostered and encouraged in early years settings. This will be followed by a book about toddlers (defined as those children aged roughly between two and three years old) and then preschool children (those aged between three and five). Such age separations reflect the most common groupings of children in UK early years settings with the majority of buildings laid out in such a way as to accommodate these three age ranges together as per one room for each.

The series is the work of Louise Day, an Early Childhood graduate who has dedicated her career so far to the development and learning of young children in her family-owned childcare setting. Her interest in the arts started at a young age, studying throughout school and carrying her interest into higher education where she exhibited her own work throughout her college years. Combining her love of art and mixed media with her passion for early years, she spends her days exploring, investigating and sharing her knowledge with groups of young children. The series is based on her interest primarily in the development of creativity but also the impact it can have in later childhood and beyond if children have not been allowed to develop their own ideas about what creativity should be or what it looks like through mindful provocations and discoveries.

Acknowledgements

I would like to take this opportunity to thank all those who contributed their ideas and inspirations and allowed me permission to use photographs of their beautifully creative settings and invitations to learning. It would not have been possible to get the breadth of examples without you all.

- Elizabeth Jarman – Founder of the Communication Friendly Spaces Approach

- Stone Hen Childcare
  - Laura Brothwell

- Reflections Nursery and Small School
  - Martin Pace

- Nina's Nursery High Lane
  - Amanda Redwood, Charlotte Blackburn and Katie Davies

- Shiny Stars Day Nursery and Shiny Stars Day Nursery Trentham
  - Alishia Woodward and Bianca Johnson

- Ronnie's Pre-School
  - Veronica Green, E.C.E., B.P.E.

- Love of Learning LLC
  - Ashley Corcoran

- Carlene's Cubbyhouse Family Day Care
  - Carlene Cox-Newton

- Squirrels Family and Childcare Centre, Northampton
  - The staff tribe and squirrels families

■ Your Nursery Ltd

■ Curiocity Childcare

■ Bright Stars Nursery

Thanks also to the wonderful parents at Wally's Day Nursery for the opportunity to work every day with your precious little babies. We have had the most fun in putting together the activity pages. Of course, to the children who made it all possible and to the staff, Emma, Iwona and Sue, our babies are lucky to have you advocating the best for them every single day. You brought fun, imagination and most of all creativity to everything we did. I am grateful to Jessica, who was wonderful enough to catch our magic moments on camera, and I'd like to thank Lone, who was always on hand with helpful journals and advice.

Special Thanks

To my own children, Theiah and Myllo, for being my inspiration and providing infinite smiles and laughter. To my parents, Elaine and Keith, for providing endless encouragement, support and, of course, sleepovers when deadlines were looming.

Most of all, I want to thank my husband, Martin, for the love and support you gave throughout and for the hot cups of tea. I couldn't have done it with you.

Contact: discover.creativity@outlook.com
Facebook: @discovercreativity2020
Instagram: @discover_creativity2020

Introduction

The ability to be creative is an important part of human development. It involves a range of skills that need to be utilised in order to create something original, and as Compton et al. (2010:8) state, 'it is present in all children. It is an attribute that can be developed and encouraged but not really taught'. It stands to reason that, as early years educators, we should facilitate as much as possible and from an early age an exploratory impulse that allows babies and young children the opportunities to explore, investigate, wonder and be inquisitive, using all of their senses in a way that will allow them to develop the skills to be creative thinkers not only in the present moment but also in the future.

I have always been interested in the development of young children, growing up in and out of settings within a military family, often following my mum wherever she worked and having the opportunity to get to know hundreds of children and families over the years. Interacting with a variety of cultures and ways of living gave me my first insight into what working with young children was all about. When our family finally found their forever home in the southwest of England, my parents started up their own setting, and I began my journey into working within the early years. In a sense, I always knew I'd end up working with children and their families and spending every day of my working week alongside some of the most honest, funny and open-hearted human beings. Sharing their learning with them is something I wouldn't trade. Despite the rising pressures of working within the sector, the constant reminder and regulation of Ofsted, staff and child retention, crippling costs of maintaining high-quality care and the changing legislations and curriculum frameworks, it is a rewarding profession that I am proud and passionate to be a part of, but I am also very aware that not everyone starts out like this. For some like myself, I believe a job in early years is a vocation, much more than just a job but a passion to care for young children and guide them in their earliest years. There are those who started working in early years because it was convenient at the time but found a love for early education and stayed, and then there are those who stay in the profession out of convenience, as a way to work certain hours and pay the bills (although most in the sector would agree there are definitely other jobs that would pay the bills and not be as stressful).

It doesn't really matter how you came to be in the position you're in today, your experiences or your qualifications, what matters is that you're here, making a difference every day to the youngest children in our early years settings.

> As Early Childhood Professionals, we are in a privileged position, we are the changemakers and educators who are shaping the future. Working with children is wonderous, challenging, magical and hard work and learning how to truly relax and get involved in children's play is wonder-full and beautiful. Take off your shoes, immerse yourself in a puddle alongside a small child, observe a bee landing on a flower, marvel at the bluest blue of the sky, tell a story about a ladybug that went on an amazing adventure. Sing and dance and get messy and play. How lucky are we to get to do these beautiful and inspiring things every day? (Carlene Cox-Newton).

It is my hope that this book will support and maybe even inspire your journey, whether you are starting out in early years and are interested to find out more about this fascinating age group and how you can be an integral part of their learning and development or if you are a practitioner or manager with years of experience, just looking for a fresh text for bedtime reading. It is important that those staff who work with babies, and indeed anyone who is interested in the care of young children, have as much information about this unique and interesting age group as possible.

Whilst researching background literature for this book, it became apparent that there is very little information available that focusses primarily on young children. We know that the first five years are crucial to a child's future life chances; however, literature focusing on very young children is somewhat shockingly lacking. This is echoed by Clare (2012) and Goouch and Powell (2013), who both suggest that the earliest years have been left out of many educational texts. This is changing though. There are several published reports that provide evidence of the importance of the first two years of life and even more specifically the impact that the experiences our young children are having both in and out of the home can have on growing brains (Field, 2010). Such reports have led to a wider reconsideration of the way we structure our early years settings and what we offer for young children. Research and work with babies is also desperately lacking, and this is more than likely due to the ethical issues that arise when working with such young children, who it is argued cannot understand consent or intent.

There is a growing body of work that has begun to put the focus back on baby rooms and the practitioners that work within them, and we will touch on the important work of the Baby Room Project (2009–2012) as we explore the important role of baby room staff in not only promoting children's creative development but also on the overall experience of young children and their families in these unique settings.

Throughout this book we will explore not only some of the important issues that are raised in the care of young babies in an out-of-home context but also how these can affect the children we care for and the impact it has on their development. More specifically, it will look at the concept of creativity and how we can support and encourage its development and the barriers that still exist to ensuring we offer a holistic approach to creative development in our baby rooms.

Context

There has been an increase in concern from a political standpoint about the care and education of very young children in recent years which has impacted the way in which settings offer their services. This can be evidenced with the growing number of funded childcare places for 'around 92,000 of the most disadvantaged 2 year olds' (DFE, 2013:1). However, whilst there has been investment in the early years to a degree, the focus has been on the education of older children, those over three years old and who attend preschools and primary schools. This has led to concern that 'the historical tradition in the UK whereby young children have been viewed as the private responsibility of the family...unless there is perceived difficulty' (Manning-Morton & Thorp, 2015: 7) has continued to be upheld. As Goouch and Powell (2013:3) state, 'the care of under 2's does not attract government funding in the UK currently and therefore it is frequently the case that the least qualified members of staff are employed with this age group, who themselves feel neglected and overlooked in relation to training and professional development'. This is not the case for all nurseries and child minders, and much work has been done to raise the profiles of those working with the youngest children: awareness of mental health concerns in the workplace is at an all-time high, and settings are doing all they can to support not only their baby room staff but also the well-being of all those who work within a setting.

There are many factors to take into consideration when investigating any aspect of young children's experiences and care in early childhood settings, some of which will be explored in this book. It is important to note the historical transformation that has occurred and theoretical concerns that have arisen in recent decades. As James et al. (1998: 3) suggest, 'childhood was once a feature of parental discourse, the currency of educators and the sole theoretical property of developmental psychology'. Since then, there have been significant changes in the way that childhood is viewed, and it has been suggested that childhood is rapidly becoming 'popularised, politicised, scrutinised and analysed in a series of interlocking spaces' (James et al., 1998: 3). These concerns are echoed by Qvortrup (1985), who suggests that because of this, children and their lives are becoming increasingly separate from that of adults. It is true that our perception of children, particularly very young children, has changed over time, and we know that they are extremely capable, even very logical thinkers from birth. Even so, it is also the case for many that 'childhood is disappearing' (Mayall, 2002: 3) at an alarming rate for a number of reasons. This view is supported by Buckingham (cited in Mayall, 2002: 3), who points out that due to the imposing nature of media in the twenty-first century, children are being rushed 'too fast through what should be a carefree and innocent period of life'. There is a huge focus in our schools on targets and meeting expected levels of development, and this is in turn having a detrimental impact on the time available for our children for free, unstructured play on their terms, something which is absolutely vital in giving children the opportunity to share and develop their own ideas. This top-down approach to learning is evident throughout our education system, particularly in primary and secondary schools, and is still apparent in many preschools and nurseries across the country.

This is a very important point to make, particularly in relation to such young children and the development of their creative abilities, as there has been a huge rise in the number of electronic devices available marketed for children. There is no escaping the technologically advanced world that is rapidly developing. New technology and even better marketing techniques mean that parents are buying into educational devices for their children, and these are taking the place of quality engagement and the ability to think independently. There is a mountain of evidence that has shown the detrimental effect of too much screen time, particularly in very young children, but despite the growing awareness of the damage this could be causing our babies, parents are feeling the pressure to ensure their children are getting the best, with some failing to recognise that, in fact, this doesn't mean the latest educational app that teaches them hand-eye coordination before they can crawl or the most brightly coloured toys complete with bells and whistles, but conversation, eye contact and play with people who are important to them will give them the best opportunities to learn and grow. Not only this but the ever-changing role society has in our expectations for children is fundamentally changing the way we parent and the choices we make for our children.

Creativity is important because it encompasses skills that are seen as favourable, not only to society but also for coping with change, using our knowledge in new ways to tackle challenges and thinking in a flexible way. In her book *The Selfish Society*, Gerhardt (2010) points out that even when we think of the word childcare, it does not express the truly unique relationships that exist within out of home settings, just the physical action. For early years professionals who recognise the important part they play in raising the youngest children in society, this is the reality that we are fighting to prove wrong – that childcare is about so much more than institutions for children whose parents must work to remain financially stable, that the profession and those who choose it should be valued for the vital role it has in nurturing future generations of creative thinkers, preparing them with the vital skills they need for a future we know nothing about.

Chapter overview

Each chapter in this book represents an important part of our understanding about the lives and early care of babies and young children up to the age of two in terms of the development of creativity. In chapter 1, we will explore some of the definitions of creativity that have been developed over the years and look at the different elements that have been noted as crucial to its development in young children.

Chapter 2 will apply these definitions of creativity specifically to babies and young children and explore why it is important to support and facilitate it in the early years. From the moment their brains begin to develop in utero, babies are already making the first of billions of connections. From what they hear to what they taste, they are already making sense of their world and, once born, this learning continues at a rapid rate. The chapter will first look at the stages of early brain development and some of the skills that are acquired in the first two years of life that contribute to a baby's ability to learn new skills. It will explore some of the major milestones of the first year and how these help each baby find their place in their community and why we should be encouraging experiences that promote creative thinking in even our youngest children.

We know that young children possess attributes that are conducive to acting with agency and that with support from adults in familiar contexts they can 'fully participate in and influence matters that concern them' (Mashford-Scott & Church, 2011: 18), influenced largely by the United Nations convention on the rights of the child, hereafter referred to as UNCRC (1989). It argues that any child who has the ability to form their own views should have the right to express those views freely, and if this is to happen 'then…practice in England needs to fundamentally reshape its paradigm' (Pascal & Bertram, 2009: 253). This is an important point to touch on, and in chapter 3 we will explore what this means for babies, why it is important in nurseries and childminding settings and how we can ensure we give babies choice and the opportunity to develop their own ideas as much as possible whilst maintaining high levels of care and ensuring that their needs continue to be met appropriately.

In infants and young children, creativity manifests itself in any number of ways that will be explored throughout this book, from an early interest in the arts or music and movement to the more developed notion of creative thinking. It is no surprise to experienced practitioners that babies learn by doing, and they have their own unique blueprint for their path to developing a range of skills. They are viewing the world for the first time, and although as adults we have seen it many times before, for babies coming into childcare settings, it may be the first time they have experienced paint, sensory activities or even being outside in the grass. This coupled with some degree of separation anxiety that can appear at any time but most often around nine months of age can make it very overwhelming for young babies and children, so it is important that they form secure attachments to their caregivers in group settings as soon as possible.

The importance of adult and baby relationships in relation to the development of creativity will be examined in chapter 4, delving into those first vital bonds that are formed whilst exploring attachment theory and the work of Bowlby (1969), who was pivotal in defining what healthy attachment relationships look like and the stages of attachment we understand today. We will also look at the part this plays in laying the foundations for trusting relationships with infants and the important differences between the home environment that is created by parents and that of an early years setting and how these differences influence the way babies interact with their environment. We will explore the relationships that are formed in early years settings, underpinned by Bowlby's theory of attachment, and the important part these play in the settling-in process, particularly when young children could be experiencing separation anxiety as mentioned above. The role of the key person along with their roles and responsibilities to young babies and the desired qualities of a baby room practitioner will also be explored to ensure that we give the babies in our care the best possible start to future creative thinking.

When young babies feel safe, secure and valued in their environment, their development will increase at a rapid rate. Only when they feel safe enough in their environment and have formed strong attachments to their caregivers will they thrive, opening them up to a world of possibilities, both indoors and out, exploring and investigating the world through fresh eyes. In chapter 5 we will look specifically at creative environments. Environments that are designed with young babies in mind face many challenges unique to them which are not thought about or considered by other rooms. This chapter breaks down the development of the environment based on physical space and its potential limitations, furniture considerations, colour choice and lighting.

Moving on from this, chapter 6 explores the resources that are needed to facilitate a creative baby room, where children are free to explore meaningful playthings in their own way. Consideration is given to recyclable materials, the use of authentic resources and the way in which practitioners can support the babies' creative processes with the use of open-ended resources.

There has been a rise in the importance of understanding well-being in young children, with the pressure of our current education system and mental health awareness for both staff and children in early years. Children are spending less and less time outdoors and interacting with nature, and this is having a detrimental impact on the unstructured time they have to think creatively and be free and subsequently the way they view the world and those within it. This is guiding many in leadership roles to evaluate their practice and make improvements to their environments to ensure children and practitioners are high on their priority list and that we do everything we can to preserve our children's childhoods and creativity. Most of the research that has been done in terms of young children's well-being reflects on the need for unhurried time in nature, experiencing reality outdoors and with authentic resources rather than through screens and artificial methods. We will explore the importance of the outdoors for babies, the sensory input they receive from natural experiences and the benefits of providing regular access to the outdoors within the context of early years group settings in chapter 7.

In the second part of the book starting with chapter 8, there is a summary of the key messages I have shared throughout the book. Within the context of the Early Years Foundation Stage in the UK, chapter 8 looks at how creative play can be used to cover many aspects of learning and development and how practitioners can use the EYFS to ensure the children in their care are receiving meaningful experiences and not as a tick list of achievements. I explain briefly process art (more on this follows throughout chapters 9-12) and what we mean when we talk about activities, invitations and provocations, as understanding these terms is crucial to providing high quality experiences. In Chapters 9 through 12, I present a range of engaging and easy to prepare invitations to create and play for young babies and opportunities for practitioners and the babies they work with to explore their own ideas, thoughts and feelings through meaningful experiences.

Chapter 9 focusses primarily on personal, social and emotional development while chapter 10 includes ways to support language and communication with young babies. Most of the invitations to play or create require minimum set-up time (essential when working with young children) and can be achieved on a budget. Most settings are becoming increasingly aware of funding and budget constraints, and so it is my intention to provide cost-effective, easy and achievable ideas that will support the developing creative mind, giving children the freedom to express themselves alongside present, observing practitioners. Chapter 11 looks at physical activities, supporting fine and gross motor skills and finally in chapter 12, we look at the outdoors and how best to utilize the space you have to get the most from your environment. Each of the chapters also include links to the ways in which the activities can support young children's repeated patterns of play (schemas).

Final note

It is my hope that I have provided a valuable tool for those in the early years sector who want to further their knowledge of creativity in respect of children under the age of two. Part two features a range of stimulating activities that can be easily set up and carried out with minimum fuss, and I hope that practitioners, in doing so, will gain more confidence in their ability to interact creatively with the children in their care. It is my belief that the more we educate ourselves about the unique nature of babies and the ever-expanding and changing world we find ourselves in, the better equipped we are to provide meaningful interactions that enhance their experience of their world within our early years settings.

In recent years there has been a rise in the number of 'new' and 'innovative' approaches to early years and the care of very young children in group and home-based settings. Many of these are, in fact, not new at all but are a return to what should be the fundamental principles of high-quality care. The notion of the capable child, the importance of the environment, developing the whole person and having a child-centred approach to education and care are not new ideas and are based on well-known theorists and practices that have existed and often been forgotten as managers and owners get swept up in the demand for good-quality, Ofsted-approved settings. Many of these vital aspects have taken a back seat as settings push towards being able to show progress and attainment and put on show what their children can do for inspections. We know that this is not what is best for young children, particularly young babies. However, with the new inspection framework published (September 2019), ownership is being given back to those in management roles to make professional judgements about how and what they deliver within their service and how they choose to evidence this.

I hope that in reading this book you will gain some valuable insight into what it should be like working with and managing rooms for young babies and children. I am aware that some of what I have touched on will not be the case for all settings and, as I have mentioned and will continue to do so throughout the book, it is important that you reflect on your own pedagogy, what you believe children to be capable of, and work towards finding a model of care that works for your setting. If you are a practitioner working within a baby room, you are part of a unique group of people who are shaping the next generation of our society; you have a responsibility like no other, and it takes hard work and determination to work with such a special age group. I applaud your hard work and dedication to our babies and hope that this book gives you the opportunity to reflect on your own practice and what you offer within your work to the babies you care for and their families.

Part I

What is creativity?

The fundamental purpose of this book is to explore important aspects of baby development – more specifically, creativity and whether we can, in fact, nurture it into being. In doing so, we first must determine what we believe creativity is. This chapter will explore some of the definitions of creativity that have been used over the years and then, using these, determine which combination of them will act as the basis for the discussions throughout the book.

'Creativity' has a vast number of connotations throughout early year's pedagogy, and the pioneers of early years all have their own view of what it is and how it is developed. It is something that many aspire to have, and as adults we often hear statements such as 'I'm not a creative person' or 'she's the creative one', but what do we mean when we make these statements? Are we putting ourselves down as we consider ourselves not to possess this ability,

or are we born with a particular set of traits that allow us to develop the ability to be creative? It is difficult to define creativity, and if we knew what it was, we would readily apply it in our nurseries, schools and communities, and society would benefit greatly from the creative thinkers we would have nurtured.

Defining creativity

We touched briefly in the introduction on the complexity of defining creativity. It has, throughout the ages, been difficult to determine exactly what it is or is not, whether it is a character trait, an ability or a skill and how important it is to our lives. There are so many questions in relation to this broad subject matter, and there are many that have cast theory and opinion into the debate. It is necessary, then, especially when writing on the subject, to explore some of the common themes and beliefs around what creativity is and how it manifests itself in babies and young children.

From all the definitions of creativity that are available, it is clear that there are many aspects that are interlinked and when taken together can account for what we know about creativity. The following characteristics of creativity are taken from *Creative Learning in the Early Years*, described by Mohammed (2018: 28–29) as 'Imaginative, Purposeful, Original, Novel, Problem-Solving, Product and of Value'. The inclusion of Product within these themes is important as it makes clear that creativity is not always about the 'concrete result' (2018:29), but it is about valuing the product in whatever form that takes, something we will explore later. It is well known that children are able to paint when provided with the right materials and ample time to explore, but how can we expect them as they get older to know about all of the different techniques that are available? We know they can construct with bricks, but that doesn't mean they know how to use Modroc or plaster of Paris to create a structure; these things need to be 'learned, practised, experimented with and tried another way in order to be mastered' (2018: 31).

A more recent definition that can be applied to early years is that of Pascal and Bertram (cited in Mohammed, 2018:31) and refers to creativity as 'imaginative activity fashioned as to produce something (process or outcome) which is both original and of value'. It is this that practitioners should take and use when planning and organising activities for young children that will support their creative development, as it values both the process and the product if there is one.

Creativity and curiosity

Babies are born curious; they have a strong, almost intrinsic motivation to explore their world, the objects within it and most importantly the people they spend time with. It is 'from this innate curiosity creativity develops' (Duffy, 2010: 125). For those of us who have had children ourselves, or those working within baby rooms with the youngest children in early years settings, we can see simply by observing babies their need for freedom and the innate curiosity they display. Duffy (2010:126) suggests that this is a predisposed curiosity that is present in all babies from birth but argues that whether or not this develops 'is largely the result of the environment and interactions we experience'. She goes on to note the impact of an environment that does not value curiosity, autonomy and freedom for children and suggests that, subsequently, children who do not have access to an environment that promotes agency and expression, find it very difficult to think creatively.

Creativity and imagination

As Duffy (cited in Moyles, 2011: 124) tells us, the difficulty in creating a definition is that the term itself 'is applied to individuals, to a process and to products'. For Vygotsky, 'creative activity, based on the ability of our brain to combine elements, is called imagination' (Sharpe, 2004: 9), whereas in contrast, Winnicot argues that 'everything that happens is creative' (1971: 91). It has been shown that creativity and imagination are very closely linked and that you cannot have one without the other. In their book *Young Children's Creative Thinking*, Fumoto et al. (2012: 16) try to define creativity by using a number of 'leading contemporary theoreticians and educators', such as Robert Sternberg, Margaret Boden and Ken Robinson, who all believe that it is the process, person or product that makes up creativity. Even the Early Years Foundation Stage, which has attempted to encompass creativity into its Expressive Art and Design area of learning, recognises how complex creativity can be. The current development matters framework takes Vygotsky's idea of combining elements and imagination and has defined two aspects of learning as exploring media and materials and being imaginative, but even these are set to be removed in the updated 2020 guidance. Craft (2002) suggests two distinct types of creativity, which she calls Big C Creativity and little c creativity. In her book *Creativity and Early Years Education* (Craft, 2002), she suggests that 'in identifying and making choices a person is inevitably self-shaping; shaping one's identity and route finding by making choices' is little c creativity. It is little c creativity that is most relevant to early years children and 'involves intelligence, imagination and aspects of self-creation and self-expression…combined together into…possibility thinking' (2002: 180).

Creativity and free choice

One major facet that appears in almost all discussions regarding the development of creativity in such young children, and one that Craft (2002) echoes, is the need for free play and free choice. O'Connor (2014:4) suggests that free play is 'the essence of early learning' and that the more time children are given to choose their own play, create their own ideas and test their own theories, the more learning that stimulates creativity will happen. Children need to be given time and quality engagement with others in order to develop

their cognitive and creative abilities. Broadhead (cited in O'Connor, 2014:5) theorises that 'what distinguishes early creative developmental learning from other types of play is the child's freedom to choose and control their activities without undue interference from adults'.

This statement leaves questions for those working with young children about exactly how and when to intervene and when to sit back and observe. It also raises an important point that we will explore later about the resources and 'toys' we provide for babies at such a crucial time in their development. If what babies and young children need are open-ended resources, sticks that can be dolls or rockets, pinecones that can be apples, then why do nurseries insist on throwing money at catalogue pages? Whilst a balance of resources and experiences are important, we need to understand more about why we choose the activities and set-ups we provide for babies and whether they are helping to immerse them in creative experiences that allow them the freedom to choose how to engage with them. For babies and young children, 'the process of creativity – which includes curiosity, exploration, play and creativity – is as important (if not more so) as any product they may create' (Duffy, 2010: 125).

Can we cultivate creativity?

Aynsley-Green (2019:1) suggests that the 'government is ignoring new science about brain development in very young children which shows that the brains of babies can make thousands of new connections every minute if they are intellectually and emotionally stimulated', something which is a vital component of supporting early creative development.

Practitioners in baby rooms across the UK are vitally important in the promotion of creativity in young children, so it goes without saying that their attitudes towards art and creativity and how they believe it should be carried out will impact the types of provision they set up for young children to explore. There are an increasing number of practitioners working with babies who know the value and benefit of what is known as process art, particularly with such young children but still there are those who are continuing to use pre-drawn templates or worse, taking artwork created by the children and making it into something else. Finding the joy in art and exploring with babies is one of the most magical things we can do in our day, and the best bit is that there is no right or wrong way to do art, especially working with babies.

Vygotsky is useful here and provides an explanation for why adults may think in this way when he writes that particular skills should be 'cultivated not imposed' (Vygotsky, 1978: 118). This suggests that the ability to be creative is not a gift or talent but that it can be 'cultivated', and without that cultivation it simply does not develop. Perhaps adults who believe they lack creativity in fact never had it cultivated in childhood, therefore showing that the failure to 'cultivate' may have a large impact on their future ability for the development of creativity and creative thinking.

Caroline Sharp (2004), in her article 'Developing young children's creativity', agrees with Vygotsky and his idea of 'cultivation'. She notes that 'it is possible to encourage or indeed inhibit the development of creativity in young children' (2004:7). This supports the notion that practitioners and, in fact, all adults have a crucial role to play in supporting children if they want them to develop creativity. Sharp develops this idea further, proposing that 'adults can act as...models of creativity for children' (2004: 8). There is evidence to suggest, therefore that it is possible to encourage creativity through a wide range of media, introducing children to a variety of experiences and engaging in open-ended play that is led by the child but supported by an adult in a sensitive way. However, she goes on to say that 'adults also have the potential to stifle opportunities for creativity by being overly didactic' (Sharp, 2004: 8). The mere notion that adults can 'inhibit' or 'stifle' children's creative development is hard to comprehend; it would mean giving the child no opportunity for free thinking or expression of their own ideas, and in the long term it would have a detrimental effect. However, in his book *Playing and Reality*, Winnicot does provide some comfort with his words 'it is probably wrong to think of creativity as something that can be destroyed utterly' (1971: 91).

According to Vygotsky (cited in Lindqvist, 2003: 248), 'art releases aspects that are not expressed in everyday life'. This suggests that children, even those of a very young age, have the creative ability to express themselves and how they feel through the marks and 'art' that they create, and the idea that it can give a child an outlet to express their emotions is a strong one. It makes it all the more important that children feel their ideas are valued and can provide a valuable tool not only in looking at the child's creative abilities but also in identifying any concerns that may not be present in any other form. This is also later referred to when she states, 'Vygotsky claimed that all human beings, even small children, are creative' (Lindqvist, 2003: 249). This coincides with the earlier argument that suggested creativity could be cultivated, and it is quite refreshing to think that even with the youngest children in educational settings, adults can start to lay the foundations for later development in this area.

Discover creativity – the definition

Whilst keeping Vygotsky and other renowned theorists in mind and taking the definition of creativity originally from the NACCCE (1999: 29) that is, 'imaginative activity fashioned as to produce outcomes that are both original and of value' this book will, in the context of early years and our baby rooms in particular, use the updated definition offered by Pascal & Bertram

(2017:1) who state that creativity is 'imaginative activity fashioned as to produce something (process or outcome) which is both original and of value'.

It is this definition that will shape the ideas that are put forward throughout this book, alongside many of the characteristics of creativity that have been mentioned above to include a child's crucial need for curiosity and time to explore alongside freedom of choice and the opportunity to engage in unhurried, purposeful play.

2 Facilitating creativity and why it matters

It is clear that there isn't one clear-cut definition of creativity that can easily be applied to our thinking, but there are certain characteristics of creativity and elements that are involved that we can use when deciding how best to promote creativity in the early years. In this chapter we will explore how we can use these to ensure that we are facilitating this important skill within our early years provision with the babies we care for.

For babies the world is a new, awe-inspiring place to be explored and investigated, and their own unique, innate curiosity will guide them in the first two years of life to finding out about each and every object they encounter. Those who work with babies already know that they are inquisitive and naturally curious about the world, but the question remains, does this make them innately creative? Is it important that practitioners 'provide' creative activities for young children, or is it now commonplace understanding that everything is linked to creative development and if supported, moreover allowed, that babies will naturally develop the skills needed for creative thinking in later years?

'Creativity is one of the basic building blocks of the human species'; it engages many areas of the brain and allows children the opportunity to express themselves through media in a way that may not be possible otherwise. When children get older, 'together with the necessity to be numerate, literate and to understand the function of the world, creativity enables humans to function at their highest level' (May, 2009: 2).

Laying the foundations for creative thinking

From the moment of conception, through their time in utero and developing throughout the first year of life, babies respond and react to their environment in a variety of ways. Without interference from others, in utero, babies have already mastered some impressive skills, including the ability to differentiate between sounds, make movements with their arms and legs as they get bigger and stronger (and as space decreases) and feel pain. Once babies are born, these skills and innate abilities continue to develop in order that they can begin to make sense of the world. Babies can respond to sounds and already distinguish their mother's voice before any

other, and as soon as they are born, they begin to make vital connections between the movements they make and the sensory input they receive.

We know that babies are born ready to learn and are sociable from birth, using innate strategies to gain attention and make contact with their surroundings, but the development of the brain is far more complex. Research has shown that the early years are a crucial period for brain development, but we know that brains are not fully developed until well into the adult years. In spite of this, it is clearly evidenced that the first three years of brain development are the most important and are characterised as a time of great opportunity, rapid change and huge vulnerability. What children experience in those important first years will have a lifelong impact on the way they think, feel and react to a range of situations.

Creative adults

It seems that there is not only varying ideas on what creativity is but also how it is viewed in a wider society, and this is important when looking at the thoughts of the child in this process. As Bruce suggests in her book *Cultivating Creativity*, 'there is a tendency to believe that creativity is a gift with which only some people are born' (Bruce, 2004: 2). This is not a new concept, and it provides an important basis for looking at the importance of adults and their pre-existing ideas surrounding creativity because, already, it begs the question of whether adults who view themselves as not possessing creativity can effectively support children to develop it. Duffy (2006: 116) writes, 'adults' attitudes are crucial to the development of creativity and imagination in young children'. She goes on to suggest that 'if we do not create an atmosphere that values these areas of learning and development children will not respond'. Children are very susceptible to the mood of others, and even young children are very in tune to those adults who are familiar to them.

When we consider young babies, we need to understand that for them everything is new, and the way in which they use and manipulate objects is innately creative; since they have little experience of how things are intended to be used, they will often find ingenious ways to handle and use objects that we wouldn't have thought of. This is crucial when thinking about how best to facilitate the creation of an environment that values babies' independent explorations.

The expectations we have when working with young children are important to think about in terms of the relationships that we form with babies, how they are listened to and the value we place on their autonomy. Expecting too much or indeed too little from the babies in our care can have a detrimental effect on the development not only of creativity but also on their development in all areas of learning. Setting aside our preconceived ideas is not easy, but it is a crucial element when thinking about what we provide for babies. Having expectations that are too high results in babies who are unable to achieve as their surroundings, activities and environment are too challenging for them. They will disengage with their environment and find it very difficult to make progress. The same can happen for children who are not challenged or stimulated in their play. When we set our expectations too low, we do our babies a disservice, not giving credit for the fantastic abilities that they have and not allowing them to progress at a rate that is natural to them. When we do not challenge our babies' abilities and value what they are capable of by extending their ideas, we are sending the message that we do not trust them and that we do not value their independent choices or skills.

Here we can draw links to Vygotsky and his notion of the zone of proximal development – that is, the space between what a baby can achieve on their own without support and what they are able to accomplish when encouraged or supported by those around them (adult or child). This idea has had an impact on the way we interact with young children and should be understood as an important marker in thinking about what children are capable of.

> Never underestimate your babies. They are capable confident learners. As much as we provide a safe secure creative environment, we as early childhood educators must be conscious to give babies experiences to push their boundaries and show their full potential. I will always stand by the fact that no matter how your environment feels and looks the quality of creative teaching will come from the adult interactions especially when considering our babies. (Laura Brothwell, Stone Hen Childcare)

We know that all babies develop in the same way, hitting the same developmental milestones throughout the first two years of life (and beyond). They will all learn to roll over, walk and begin using language. But whilst we know they will all follow the same path, how they get there and the rate at which they do so will differ greatly between babies.

It is how we as practitioners respond to these differences that will have the most impact in a baby's development, and being clear about how we want to support them will help us to make the right decisions in terms of facilitating creative learning and the environments that are offered. For babies, the relationships they form in the first few months of life are the most important. Creating bonds with familiar adults leads to secure, trusting relationships within which babies are confident to explore their surroundings and engage with what is on offer. It is important then that the adults who work with babies remain

open-minded and flexible in their thinking about the creative endeavours that most babies find themselves in and that they join babies in their play.

Practitioners should be trained specifically in baby care of children up to the age of two in order to understand fully the joy but also the unique challenge that accompanies this age group and to ensure that there is underpinning knowledge to enable them to understand the needs of the babies in their care in order for them to provide the best quality.

Routines in early years

Creative behaviour can be particularly affected by restrictive routines; whilst routines of some sort do have a place in childcare settings – for example, when the children may be required to have lunch and/or rest time – they can also limit the children's ability to respond and find solutions to problems and work out new ways of doing things in their own time. They can also change the way children view particular events and the way they respond to any given task. Children who spend too much time in a restrictive environment are, as a consequence, unable to follow their own interests or self-expressions as they develop an inherent need to follow rules and be guided.

Babies are often thought of as dependent on adults for the majority of their early lives, and whilst this is the case for their care routines and ensuring their needs are met, they also need time, unhurried and free of restriction, to practice skills they have been working on or are developing. In terms of their artistic ability, too many restrictions cause it to diminish substantially, and although it may still be apparent, it will almost always take the form of an adult-directed end product. In order to stop this from happening, we need to make sure that we give babies enough time and open-ended resources to explore their own ideas and ways of doing things with helpful, well-placed comments rather than statements and without raised voices or overly protective actions.

Facilitating flexibility

Carlene Cox-Newton, founder of Carlene's Cubbyhouse Family Day Care, understands the importance of flexibility in ensuring that young children have the opportunity to make their own choices and feel 'empowered' in their learning environment. She reflects,

> The lives of today's children are rushed to the point of mania. They are carted from activity to activity, overscheduled and overstimulated. Their days are filled with sound, movement, devices and distraction. No wonder we are seeing children who are exhausted, can't sit still and children who have forgotten how to PLAY! How can you, as an influential person in a child's life, create a second home where children can relax, be themselves, play uninterrupted and get to know the world around them?

She also offers some valuable questions for practitioners to reflect on their day-to-day practices with young children:

> Does your schedule allow for long periods of play? Does it give a child time to follow their interests for extended periods of time? Does it allow flexibility of how and when a child

eats, rests, sits, listens, creates, plays? Do children have some choice or say over this matter? In a world where children have little to no say over their lives, how can you make them feel empowered, important, valued and supported?

In her own day care, a range of accessible resources, made available daily at the children's height, allows babies to exercise their autonomy and make selections independent of the adult, allowing for creative thinking to flourish.

Giving babies time

More than anything else, babies need time – time to explore what they are capable of and develop new skills when they are ready. This is perhaps the most important point of all when working with babies and young children to facilitate creativity and the development of new skills. Whilst lots of skills can be specifically taught when children reach the age of around five or six, this just is not the case for babies. For those who have been working across the ages, you know all too well that unless a child is ready, they will not master something new. To be ready means both 'growth and development must be in place before a new skill can be acquired' (Stoppard, 2005: 4), so it is vital that those working with babies understand both the mental and physical development of young children to ensure that we provide appropriately stimulating environments and invitations to share creative learning.

With routines and day-to-day practices in place, set outdoor play for many and lunch and sleep times to contend with, there is very little time dedicated to respecting babies' choices, and this needs to change. Along with treasure baskets that provide a great opportunity for independent play, 'art making is one of the most powerful places to give a child a voice in what they want and don't want' (Haughey, 2020: 13), and this time should be used wisely.

Facilitating creative activity

So far, I have used particular language centred around the types of activities that we set up for babies. If we take the view that babies are more than capable of making choices in matters that concern them, then we have to forget the idea that activities should be done to babies rather than with them. Using the language of invitations to play and provocations when we talk about what we set up and provide for babies implies respect for children's agency and gives them the chance to be invited to participate in a particular experience and, more importantly, the option not to. There is often talk amongst early childhood professionals regarding the difference between an invitation and a provocation. An invitation encourages a child to do something, creating an experience with a range of flowers, herbs, bottles and food colours invites a child to create potions of their own choosing with the materials available. A provocation is when you set up an experience that provokes a child to follow their own learning. A table with clay, sticks, feathers and loose parts will spark a child's thinking and they will investigate these materials in their own way using them how they see fit.

Both of these methods of exploring learning for children are useful when planning what we can offer babies. For a long time, these types of invitations were not available to babies, and in some nurseries they still aren't regularly accessible as many practitioners are either not confident in their own abilities to facilitate them or are concerned about the risk (particularly if loose parts are involved). We have to get past this. We need to trust ourselves to keep them safe and supervised and trust our babies to breathe life into our offerings.

When we are planning provocations and invitations to learning the children's interests are at the heart of what we do. We use this to plan outdoor experiences or bring the outdoors in, basing these experiences on their current skills and next steps of development. We focus closely on nurturing our babies and meeting their care and welfare needs at all times. Staff take each child's individual routines and work with this throughout the day, making adjustments to the day and plans accordingly. This is all documented on our intent, implementation and impact planning sheets as and when this occurs. We reflect and look back at the day and record what was planned, what happened and what impact this has had on each child present. (Squirrels Family and Childcare Centre)

Planning for creativity should therefore be minimal yet well thought out where babies are concerned, and the new inspection framework against which settings are judged by Ofsted seems to reflect this, suggesting that settings can use their professional judgement to define how they 'teach' young children and how they implement that teaching. That said, this has caused many practitioners to debate not planning at all, but that is not the best way forward.

There must be some form of planning in place, but the shape of that planning can differ hugely between settings. There has been a move over the last few years towards in-the-moment planning, championed by Anna Ephgrave as a way to engage in meaningful, child-led learning and decrease the amount of paperwork that practitioners are required to do. This is the best type of planning for babies, as it stays true to the notion of moving with the child's interests, researching their fascinations with them and extending their play in that moment rather than waiting for an appropriate time, which in the case of babies may never come. It is important that babies are respected and the many ways in which they learn are honoured too. Schematic play is a huge part of a baby room as young children are learning all the time about how objects work and what they can do with them. Athey (2006) describes how young children's learning is often linked to one or more schemas, and therefore these should be incorporated into daily invitations to explore and learn more about what they can do, and planning on a day-to-day, moment-by-moment basis is the best way to facilitate this.

REFLECTION

■ What do you already do to promote creativity in the baby room?

■ In a group, choose an area of your room and discuss the creative possibilities it facilitates.

Respectful planning for supporting creativity

In order to facilitate early creativity, it is vital that we reflect on the processes we have in place that enable us to plan for babies. To take the view that babies can fully participate in matters that concern them is to understand what that means for those who work with them and how it is translated into some of the practice that is evident in baby rooms across the country. Planning and observation must be adapted, as activities would no longer be provided *for* babies based on what *we* believe they want or their level of development, often pushing them too far before they are ready, but *with* them, based on *their* interests (evidenced through meaningful observations), fascinations and ability level (which varies widely between babies), something which many settings are beginning to take on board and adapt accordingly.

In terms of developing a creative mind, this is a positive step in allowing the very youngest children the opportunity to exert some control over what they participate in, but it still relies heavily on experienced practitioners knowing each baby's particular cues and watching their body language for signs they want to withdraw and take some time for reflection or solitary play. The floor book approach to planning is particularly helpful in noticing and respecting infant voices.

Good-quality observational skills can take years to develop; even for experienced practitioners, it can be difficult to step back and trust the babies in their care to make choices. To some, it is a fine tightrope that must be walked in order to fully develop our own worldview of babies and their capabilities. How practitioners plan and provide experiences to support the development of creativity in the youngest children is vital. Throughout this book there are examples of good practice from a wide range of settings, some home-based childcare and other, larger organisations. There is one common theme that can be seen among their differences, though, and that is whatever their choice of format for planning and observation, the child is at the centre.

As baby rooms in group settings often lead on to the rest of the nursery and eventually preschool education, it is these environments, early interactions with the world and relationships that provide the foundation for later learning. This poses some difficulty in planning for babies as the expectations of those working with older children, particularly those who receive the children when they reach the next stage of their learning, may be limiting. It is easy for practitioners to be swept up in the demand for the children in the baby room, these innately curious babies, to have skills designed for the next stage in their learning. Instead of practitioners focusing on the here and now of enjoying the world alongside babies, allowing them all the opportunities to build skills at their pace and practise what they are learning on their terms, often carers will be reminded that they 'should' be supporting babies to reach the next milestone so they are 'ready' for the next room, often forgetting that each child will develop the necessary skills in his or her own time.

Redefining observation and assessment

Too often in nurseries in the UK, managers and practitioners are concerned with tracking the development of the children, what they are learning and the rate at which they are progressing. This is the reality for many settings; however, it goes against some of the fundamental theories of early education and the development of children that we have come to understand. It is important for those working with babies to know where the children are developmentally. This supports planning and resourcing for children who may be finding particular skills difficult and can help to provide early interventions for those who need it.

For some practitioners, though, their days are consumed with whether a child is reaching their milestones at the right time. Perhaps the rest of the group has mastered a skill that one child is finding difficult, or they haven't written anything down yet this week, so they hope one of their key children does something in line with the early years foundation stage so they can make a note and record it. Working in a baby room shouldn't be like this. As the saying goes, they are only little once, and baby room practitioners have a unique opportunity to share in some of a baby's first discoveries. Slowing down, watching and observing babies without a preconceived idea of what should happen next allows practitioners to perceive the world from a baby's point of view. After all, babies are not interested in when they learn to roll, babies have no concept of time; they are concerned only with the idea that they can do it, and they will do it if given the time, opportunity to explore their body and supportive, mindful adults who share their space and are ready to engage with them.

TOP TIPS FOR REFLECTION AND FACILITATING CREATIVE PLANNING/ASSESSMENT

- Reflect on your current planning processes:
    - Do they meet the needs of the children?
    - Are they based on the children's current interests and fascinations?
    - Does planning complement what you believe about the care of young children?

- Ensure you have routines that allow children plenty of opportunity for free play on their terms.

- Are you flexible in applying these routines, or are they time specific?

- Try removing the clock in your room for a day and see how this changes the flow of activities.

- Take your cues for changes from the babies in your care instead of the time on the clock.

- Ensure planning reflects the children and their development rather than what they should be achieving next.

■ Consider your current assessment process:

- Who is it for?

- What purpose does it serve?

- What evidence is required, and is it all needed?

■ Think about your displays, if these feature annotated photographs, comments and examples of the children's mark making – is there a need to then rewrite them as part of formal assessment for babies?

■ Remember: Always meet them where they are, not where you think they should be.

TEAM ACTIVITY

Give each member of staff a small piece of paper and a pen. Individually, write down one word or sentence that describes your approach to supporting creativity.

Take it in turns to share your sentence and discuss how this is reflected in your day-to-day practice. What improvements could you make?

Disposing of the 'conveyor craft mentality'

Let's revisit process art and mess for a minute, which, in my opinion, should be the only way to do art with babies. Process art is 'all about the making and the doing rather than the finished product' (Cherry, 2019: 7), and mess or 'playing with extremes' (Hobson, 2019:1) is so important in telling children we value their efforts and their thinking and leaves no space for preconceived ideas. The structure of the early years foundation stage in the UK makes it easy to assume that the arts and creativity are the same thing, but this is not the case. And just because the heading 'expressive arts and design' encompasses creativity, it is not a given that the two will coexist.

Many art experiences offered to babies in nurseries are 'dull, repetitive and far from creative' (Duffy, 2010: 127); think hands and footprints or paper plate activities facilitated by adults and you're halfway there. Many practitioners prefer this way of working because it is predictable, less messy, easy to manage and plan for and over in less than ten minutes. The babies, on the other hand, do not prefer this. Whilst they may appear compliant, there is no real joy, and whilst they may appear happy, there is no freedom of expression. There are no smiles or squeals of delight from having your hand painted by an adult then held to a piece of paper before it is removed and wiped off, ready for you to go and play. What is effectively a conveyor belt of activity usually for the adults' or parents' benefit is not what babies (or, in fact, any children) need.

It is hard; and for those who feel they may be part of what I call the conveyor craft system, often it is not your fault entirely. I would always advocate for standing up for what you believe. If you think there is a better way, then please, speak to colleagues; they may feel the same. Have a professional discussion with your manager and share your concerns and ideas for a better way. Your babies depend on you to make things better and bring the joy and love of art back into the baby room. The hard part is often parents' expectations, and we have probably all experienced this at some time in our careers. Parents like cards and gifts, to get something special from their little one at important times of the year that says 'I love you, Mummy', and to be honest, they probably don't mind the handprint Christmas tree or the footprint rabbit at Easter. What parents see is a cute handprint or footprint; they don't see the process by which it was achieved. As practitioners, we often don't want to be empty-handed, and this expectation often means we revert back to conveyor crafts.

Like many things, it is easier just to keep on going because that's the way it has always been done, but that is not what is best for our babies. If we have any chance of encouraging creative thinking, we need to stop and take stock of what we are doing. I am not suggesting that we have to stop sending cards home, but even babies, as we have seen, are more than capable of independently making marks in a variety of ways. As a parent myself, I love getting a card at Christmas or a handmade gift on Mother's Day; I am the same as every other mum in that respect. The difference is that I appreciate it much more when I know my child made it themselves, when they chose the colours, the materials and where to stick their resources or place their brushstrokes. Many children in early years are still being sent home with paintings that they have created when, in fact, they didn't create it at all; it is, in fact, a 'tribute to the artistic talent of the practitioner and has nothing to do with the baby' (Clare, 2012: 83). This matters because we are sending subliminal messages to our babies about the importance we place on these types of experiences. If we want our children to be the creative thinkers of the future, we need to support them in their earliest years.

Furthermore, before we delve into the wonder that is process art, it is important to explore the notion that, generally speaking, it is adults that stand in the way of a young child's creativity in a number of ways, and it needs to stop if we are to truly honour the children's ideas and get the best from them. In early years settings, there are a number of practitioners who don't like the mess (or the thought of cleaning it), and it is because of this that they try to stop young children in their creative attempts, particularly when doing art. Step back and ask whether the child is doing anything wrong. Are they going to get hurt or hurt another child? If the answer is no, I implore you to have a go at the 'why not?' philosophy. If the practitioner has taken the necessary steps to prepare (as much as is possible when working with babies), then try asking 'why not?' Why can't they do that, paint there, touch that? What harm or damage are they doing? If the answer is none, then take a second and watch; observe the magic as it happens.

Engaging children in creative thinking

As Sharp (2004:6) states, 'view children in their earliest years as highly creative, with a natural tendency to fantasise, experiment and explore their environment', and share this with them. We can support children in a number of ways with open-ended questioning, commenting and modelling what to do with different tools or techniques. Babies are master imitators and will copy adults and watch for reactions. Enjoy art making with young children, and comment using

'I wonder' (yes, even to babies), as this will 'draw the children's attention to possibilities but not put them under pressure' to do it your way.

Something that goes hand in hand with the 'why not?' philosophy is the idea of creating a 'yes space' for children. This is a space that encompasses everything we have talked about so far with regard to facilitating creativity in young children and them having autonomy and choice in their environment, free from the preconceived ideas of the adults that work with them:

> A 'Yes' space is a space where children are free to play without constant direction and guidance. It is a space where children choose the how, what, where, when of their play and are empowered by their own decisions. These spaces are important for older children but are ESSENTIAL for babies and toddlers. A yes space gives a small child the freedom to explore and build on all their emerging developmental skills. New and exciting things do not need to be made available to this age group every day; predictability and providing an environment that supports and nurtures are what matters most here. Set up low tables with things children can have access to and expect them to be carted all around your setting! Please don't expect to have 'perfect' activities set up all the time. Expect paint to be licked, playdough to be mouthed, and things to end up on the floor. Approach the environment as if it is a teacher alongside you and provision it accordingly. Think about how often you have to redirect young children from an area, if it is constant and the children are not using it appropriately, then the environment needs to change…not the children. A 'yes' space is exactly that, a space where you rarely have to redirect or say 'no'. Think about whether your space allows for lots of 'yes' to occur and if it doesn't, how can you make it a little bit more user friendly for children? (Carlene Cox-Newton)

Process art

'For creativity to thrive, it is essential for the creative child to be actively engaged' (Mohammed, 2018: 57). It is this that provides the perfect starting point for process art exploration with babies and young children because in the early years the importance should be placed on the 'processes that children engage with in their learning environment, which are not necessarily outcome based; the outcome is the child's choice to make' (Mohammed, 2018: 31). In a nutshell, the importance in process art is the process. The experience and engagement of the child is much more important than any end product that evolves, and for babies it is the perfect type of art and the only type that matters.

Since babies do not plan ahead, they can't possibly know how an idea or project will turn out, and in that sense process art was made for babies and babies are the best at it. This is something that practitioners can struggle with. They often think they need to show a baby what to do or how to do something and do not respect the autonomous opportunities that arise from this type of play and 'because they feel they are not supporting the babies unless they are interacting, they intervene and frequently take over' (Clare, 2012: 85). Lots of the ideas in part 2 are based on this idea of process over product. When we think about babies and their autonomy, still in early years settings they are not given enough of a say over what happens to them.

There is no better time to introduce art than when children are very young, and the more we allow them to experiment, the more likely they are to grow into children who feel they are valued enough to create in a way they choose, not that is chosen by the adults around them. This can start as soon as babies show an interest in mark making or even before. It will depend on your own ideas about when babies are 'old enough' to make art or even attempt to explore some of the materials, but there are lots of edible paints and doughs that can be offered from around six months (some of these are detailed in part 2), and it doesn't always have to be messy. If you are new to the process art tribe, then start with something manageable, perhaps with a dough or a dry mix and mess, providing a range of dry ingredients and small pots and spoons for babies to mix, fill, empty and pour.

Once you are a little more confident and have begun to see the wonder and curiosity that is sparked from such activities, you could begin to add small amounts of coloured water and progress to paint, shaving foam, clay and many more opportunities. An important aspect of process art or 'wonder art' that is perfect for babies and their emerging schematic interests is that 'inside each wonder-based art project is an underlying process that captures the child's

interest' (Haughey, 2020: 18). Whether a baby enjoys filling and emptying, throwing or knocking things down only to rebuild them, there is some form of process that can be facilitated in order to explore these patterns of play through art, so it is worth observing the interests of the children and incorporating these into an invitation to create. Babies are much more likely to engage in activities that catch their attention and excite them.

REFLECTION

■ What elements of process art do you use in your provision?

■ If you don't currently facilitate process art, reflect on what you do and whether there is need for improvement or adjustments you could make.

Supporting creative thinking in other ways

It is important to remember that it is not always about art and making things. Creativity manifests itself in a number of ways, and each one can be supported and developed by knowledgeable practitioners in almost any area of the curriculum. Extending on a child's existing knowledge and interests is crucial to providing a range of experiences that will challenge and stimulate their thinking and allow babies to explore in their own way. At Stone Hen Childcare, Laura provides her babies with the opportunity to investigate and explore in creative ways, especially with everyday objects:

Babies are naturally curious. We love to give our babies the opportunity to investigate and explore, especially with everyday objects (please don't forget to risk assess before).

Technology, Lights and Shadows, provide babies with great benefits such as improving problem solving and cognitive skills to enhancing creative thinking and self-expression. Such creative opportunities give babies a great sense of empowerment and confidence that they are capable learners.

When we think about what we know about babies and their innate desire to learn and explore, it stands to reason that this type of resource is worth its weight in gold to the growing mind as babies use all of their senses to investigate the objects

that are provided for them. Careful observation ensures that practitioners are able to pick up on emerging interests and enhance their babies' creative learning opportunities.

The important thing to remember is that it doesn't have to take a long time to set up or prepare. We all know that babies would be quite happy playing in a cardboard box rather than with what was in it or with the remote control to the television. Take their lead and allow them the opportunity to explore real-life items. Stimulating a baby's creativity and interest doesn't have to be difficult. If we keep in mind the idea that babies are learning about the world through their senses and want to find out about the properties of objects and test their theories, we can offer almost anything (within reason and subject to risk assessment) to ignite their curiosity. A multitude of learning can easily be achieved by adding to provision already in place, upcycling other items and repositioning furniture.

Turning a cot on its side provides another perspective for young children to explore and an opportunity to test their physical skills as well as having somewhere to rest and recharge in an enclosed space. Using babies' favourite books and providing provocations to deepen their understanding with resources they can touch, feel and experience whilst extending babies' current fascinations will also add to their

experience. By adding resources to particular areas regularly or setting the scene for babies at different times of the year, such as in the spring or at wintertime, babies experience a wide range of opportunities that might not ordinarily be available.

Many practitioners dedicate long hours to the profession in the hope that they can make a difference to the lives of the babies in their care. By setting up different invitations that complement all areas of learning, they can be sure that as long as they are facilitating the key elements that are essential for creative thinking, they are supporting their babies through the activities they offer. It is very easy to make cross-curricular links with the early years foundation stage, and most baby room staff understand the importance of doing so when supporting babies.

Simple activities such as adding props to stories or ensuring a multisensory approach to singing or story time with instruments, coloured ribbons and puppets can lend itself readily

to increased participation and excitement, especially for young babies who are learning how their body moves and those older babies who are beginning to move in response to stimuli they enjoy.

> We love to provide our babies with inspiring literacy enhancements. Helping them to link their favourite books into multi-sensory experiences, developing their understanding and giving endless opportunity to develop speech and creative thinking. (Laura Brothwell - Stone Hen Childcare).

The carers at Squirrels Family and Childcare Centre in Northampton also understand the importance of offering young children enhancements to their environment to ensure a holistic approach to not only literacy but also learning in all areas in order to facilitate creativity. Books are provided alongside authentic, natural resources and dough to allow the children the opportunity to experiment with making marks and creating sculptures. Babies benefit from a range of related text and print alongside their activities to support their understanding.

The impact that the environment and what happens within it has on our babies is profound, and failure to provide a range of exciting, stimulating, sensory-rich experiences for our youngest children alongside meaningful interactions can have a devastating impact on their future learning and creative ability. Without adults to support them and scaffold their learning, whilst ensuring that they have ample time to explore freely without interruption, children will not be able to develop the necessary skills that are vital for creative thinking.

3 Pioneering influences

When it comes to looking after babies, we all have our own core beliefs and values. These are most likely based on the way we were brought up, the babies we have encountered and our own observations of others, perhaps watching parents in supermarkets or from our experiences in settings. Whatever inspired us and however we came to them, our beliefs and values are our own, and they will inevitably be slightly different to those of people around us. So how is that possible, and how does it affect the way we care for babies in early years provision? In this chapter we will explore some of the most influential philosophies that have shaped the way we think and feel about the care of young children and how this has manifested itself. We will also look at how settings can create a cohesive model that every member of staff working with the youngest children can both agree on and adhere to whilst maintaining the highest level of care for the babies they look after every day. It will look at where our ideas about how we care for babies come from, the influences that affect them and how we can work together to combine what is considered essential in terms of high-quality care for infants whilst also keeping in mind the necessary regulatory bodies and statutory guidance that exists in the UK.

Our view of the child

In developing a view of children that sees them as social beings who are competent and active in their environments, it is important that the concept of childhood is explored briefly. The view that children are 'inadequately socialised future adults' (James & Prout, 1997: xiv) is still prominent in the debate surrounding childhood and is heavily relied on by politicians who appear largely uninterested in young children (Kagan et al. cited in Dahlberg et al., 2013: 47) in terms of the agenda for early years. However, a shift in thinking has taken place in recent decades away from 'the dominance of the fragile child position' (Sommer, 2012: 18) and the view that the child is a novice as opposed to a competent individual. This is particularly important in relation to such young children, as this has led to a 'growing acknowledgement of infants' ability to develop in a socially expanding world' (Sommer, 2012: 17).

Theories concerned with social learning have been influential in the understanding of knowledge and the extent to which young children are treated as 'passive recipient[s]' (Sommer, 2012: 23) within their environment. This view has been endorsed by early theories surrounding socialization and the importance of the family; however, there has been criticism of these ideas, as they have 'no theoretical consideration for the eventual positive/negative impact of experiences that infants encounter in contexts *outside the family*' (Sommer, 2012: 15). These theories are based on the idea that children, in order to become social beings, need to be socialized within family groups; however, more recent research has begun to acknowledge that 'there are developmental benefits of high quality early childcare and education' (Sommer, 2012:59).

The concept that early education has an impact on future development is largely known, and good quality care and education for young children has many benefits for future outcomes. This implies a link to the idea of children as 'human capital and social investment' put forward by Kjørholt (2013: 245). The very real concern here, in the context of early years, is that even very young children, when considered as human capital, are overlooked as individuals in favour of what they may become. The 'human becoming conception of childhood perceives children as passive actors' (Peleg, 2013: 526) similar to the suggestion made by Sommer (2012) and Lee (2001: 8), who have argued that children have historically been seen only as 'dependent and passive recipients of adults actions'. Peleg (2013: 526) argues that in this view, children are 'lacking agency, weak, vulnerable and in need of protection', but in contrast, we now know that children are, in fact, active agents who are more than able and willing to learn from birth and should be treated as such.

On closer examination of the Nordic countries, it is clear that they have a very different outlook on what it means to be a child and the very construction of childhood. Despite the fact that these countries have 'many of the same issues…regarding childhood and childhood education' (Einarsottir & Wagner, 2006: viii) that countries in the west experience, the way they have responded to them is intrinsically different and something that should be noted. One major difference is the appreciation the Nordic countries have for the 'nature of childhood itself' (Einarsottir & Wagner, 2006: viii). They place emphasis on the quality of childhood, whereas here in the UK, government policy concerning the education of children focusses much more on 'play as a means to learning academics' (Spodek cited in Einarsottir & Wagner, 2006: vii). This idea is echoed by Woodhead (2006), who suggests that historically children in the UK were seen as a means to a better economy and thought of in terms of what they could offer society, rather than education being a tool to unlock individual potential. This is relevant not only because it suggests young children are being 'primed' for adult life prematurely but also because it places increased pressure on early years practitioners to maintain the innocence and wonder of childhood whilst meeting demands for assessment and progress checks on even our youngest children.

There have been many ideas regarding childhood throughout the twentieth century, and the constructions of the child that are evidenced by Dahlberg, Moss and Pence (2013: 47) seem to provide an accessible account of how children are thought of. They describe how these particular constructions of the child have 'influenced the whole childhood landscape' (Dahlberg, Moss & Pence, 2013: 47), placing the child either as 'starting life with and from nothing' or as 'innocent and primitive' (Dahlberg, Moss & Pence, 2013: 49). New constructions, emerging for a variety of reasons both social and political, describe the child as a 'co-constructor from the very start of life' (Dahlberg, Moss & Pence, 2013: 53). Children are now beginning to be recognized much more widely as being able to participate in their own learning. They do not 'passively endure their experiences but become active agents' (Rinaldi, 1993: 105) and are able to be in society as 'social actors, participating in constructing and determining their own lives but also the lives of those around them' (Dahlberg, Moss & Pence, 2013: 52). This means, according to Dahlberg, Moss and Pence (2013: 54), 'the young child is not only included, but in active relationships with society and the world', a point echoed by Pugh and Duffy (2014: 97) when they add that children are 'people in their own right and as such should be recognized as socially active participants'.

The Plowden report

The notion of children as active learners and the publishing of the Plowden report in 1967 inspired many settings in the UK to adopt a more child-led approach to their planning and daily routines with young children, although there is still much debate about whether this way of working is being implemented effectively (Goouch & Powell, 2013: 47). Based on the fundamental belief that children are active in their learning, innately curious, creative and social from birth, the report rightly states that 'at the heart of the educational process lies the child' (Central Advisory Council for Education, 1967:7), something which we need to keep at the forefront of our work with young children.

We do know that there has been a shift in thinking in terms of when 'learning' begins. Where it was previously thought this only happens once a child starts formal education, we know quite confidently that this is not the case and that children are learning from the moment they are born and almost certainly to some extent throughout their lives. The 'process of learning and development then is continuous and culminates rapidly' (Mohammad, 2018: 43), which is why it is important to 'start developing creativity early' and ensure that practitioners understand how to support and scaffold children's learning as it occurs.

Pioneering ideas

I have already touched on the growing trend in the UK for settings to follow a particular ethos or well-known ideal about how infants and young children should be cared for within early childhood settings. There are many approaches to childcare and early education that are now widely accepted and implemented in a range of ways across the globe, and the implementation of the new inspection framework in 2019 makes it possible for settings to design their own curriculum and the pedagogy that makes their setting and the children within it stand out. From the earliest theorists who developed ideas on early childhood education, learning and development, the experiences of young children have always been at the forefront of thinking. Naturally the ideas of the first have somewhat changed over the years as thinking develops, new ideas are brought to the forefront and different ways of working with young children are tried and tested. However, there is one key aspect of them all that remains constant, and that is the idea that children should be central to the learning process.

There are always buzz words in early years and, of course, fad responses to an apparent need or problem that will come and go; many are based not on new ideas but on the fundamental building blocks of what we know about child development, which are then woven in with a setting's own ideas and beliefs. Below I have provided a brief overview of some of the founding theories of education. Of course, this is not an exhaustive list, but I have included those who I believe have been the most influential when thinking about babies and their learning.

Friedrich Frobel (1782–1852)

Froebel had a lot of offer the world of education. He is credited with developing the term *Kindergarten* (Pound, 2011: 12) and had an interest in nature, which led to a relatively romantic view of early education. 'His notion of the child as an integral part of nature who should be left to blossom is indicative of his romantic view of the kindergarten and his belief that it is nature, not nurture that is the basis of human development' (Pound, 2011: 13).

With a focus on play and spirituality, he advocated for 'the idea that education should take account of the child's natural interests and stage of development' (Millar, 1968: 14). This is a returning theme in early years, as we are seeing more and more settings move away from themes and topics when planning for children in favour of interest-based child-led activities and routines. Like many that followed, Frobel believed that children were creative, and his work encouraged the 'notion that learning essentially comes from doing' (Pound, 2011:13). With his interest in play, his theories are relevant even today, as it is through play (an inherently creative activity) that we know the most connections and new learning are made.

Rudolf Steiner (1861–1925)

The theories underpinning much of Steiner's philosophy to education have been outlined in the document *Guide to the Early Years Foundation Stage in Steiner Waldorf Early Childhood Settings* (2009: 5). His approach is described as 'the interdependence of physical, emotional, social, spiritual and cognitive development. It takes account of the whole child, including his/her soul qualities and believes that children's learning flourishes in a calm, peaceful, predictable, familiar and unhurried environment that recognises the child's sensory sensitivities'. The idea that we should be focussing on the whole child is still relevant today, as it is well known that children develop best when they are cared for in a holistic way, focussing not only on the intellectual skills necessary for the next stage in their development but also on other important aspects that are considered the foundations for future achievements.

In terms of what this philosophy could look like for children in today's early years settings, there should be a 'calm and purposeful atmosphere', as this was 'highly valued' (Pound, 2011: 36), along with a focus on the natural world, much like the authentic resources that we are seeing returning to our provision. Observation plays a huge role in Steiner's theory. Keeping the child at the centre, it is referred to not as observation but as 'picture building' (Pound, 2011: 38), and instead of a focus on reading and writing at an early age, children are not introduced to print or technology until much later. Something we can only dream of in today's society.

Similar to other views on the environment, for Steiner it was seen as of high importance, and creating a space for children where they can feel nurtured and at ease was important. 'The quality of sound is that of human voices rather than mechanical toys. The materials in the room are natural and are at children's level and stored in aesthetic containers such as simple baskets or wooden boxes' (Drummond et al, 1989: 59). If your baby room features any of these considerations, then you can consider yourself inspired by the work and theory of Steiner. It is clear that through our own practices, 'the greatest legacy of Steiner's theories is the fact that they have endured' (Pound, 2011: 39).

Maria Montessori (1870–1952)

Another great theorist whose ideas have endured the test of time is Maria Montessori. Her main thoughts with regard to child development centred around the idea that there are sensitive periods when a child is more likely to learn particular skills effectively. If these periods are missed, the child may be unable to learn the skills, which include language, coordination of senses and socialisation (Bradley cited in Pound, 2011: 42). She also believed in freedom of choice and independence for children, something which many settings are now striving for.

The range of resources that have been developed to fit with the prescriptive methods of teaching are used not only by Montessori settings but also by a range of other types of provision and are often made of wood and aesthetically pleasing, much like that of Steiner's ideas. Life skills are highly valued in Montessori education, and children engage daily with cooking, gardening and cleaning, learning skills that will support them in the long term. These skills are particularly relevant now as settings in the UK become accustomed to the term 'cultural capital', recently introduced (although not a new idea) to ensure that children in all early years settings are given the knowledge, experiences and opportunities to develop a wide range of skills that will be needed throughout their lives.

Lev Vygotsky (1896–1934) and Jean Piaget (1896–1980)

The legacy left by both Vygotsky and Piaget underpins most of what we know today about early childhood and is linked to many areas of the early years foundation stage. Piaget is widely known for his contributions to our knowledge relating to the stages of development that children go through.

Linked to intellectual development, Piaget put forth that each stage was directly linked to a particular age (as is our current early years foundation stage layout). 'Piaget saw the child as constantly constructing and reconstructing reality – achieving increased understanding by integrating simple concepts into more complex ones at each stage' (Pound, 2005: 37). He also identified four stages that applied to all children. For the purpose of this book, it is the sensorimotor stage that is most important, for children aged birth to two years old. In this stage, he suggests that children learn through sensory experiences and physical action (that is, the process of doing). Interestingly though, and despite the current format of the curriculum in the UK, Piaget has not been linked to developing an educational theory. Egan (1983:123) argues that 'the function of an educational theory is to tell us how to design a curriculum which will produce educated people, or rather lay out such a curriculum'. Piaget did not do this; he was interested in psychology and 'developing understanding of children's conceptual development and understanding', but his work did not have 'educational application' (Pound, 2011: 109).

Vygotsky, on the other hand, concentrated on the 'child as social and communicative' (Cohen, 2002:59), something which Piaget did not seem to focus on. For Vygotsky, children are a product of their social context, and he believed that the community around the child plays a huge part in the meaning-making ability of the child. His notion of the zone of proximal development has been influential in early years practice and has helped to develop the idea that scaffolding is crucial to young children's cognitive development. The age and stage theory is still prevalent in the modern-day approach to early years, continually looking for the areas that children have achieved in order to move them on, but despite this there is a growing number of professionals that are beginning to fight back and advocate for a more child-led approach to development.

Emmi Pikler (1902–1984)

A well-known name in the world of baby care and respectful relationships with infants is Emmi Pikler. Piker is known for her revolutionary approach to the care of infants and makes respectful interaction and free movement a priority. The relationship between the

nurse and the infants is formed in a planned way while she is caring for the children and not through the use of so-called organised activities. Like the ideas of other theorists, Dr Pikler advocates for peaceful, trust-filled relationships that acknowledge the infant as free and equal. She posits that 'infants who actively participate in their daily care and are emotionally balanced are also active and full of initiative beyond the care situation' (Pikler, 1979:5). She goes on to add that infants and children who are brought up this way do not demand the same amount of help from adults in later years.

Pikler is well known for her ideas regarding physical development, later written about extensively by Magda Gerber, a student of Pikler's. Gerber argues that babies should not be put in positions that they cannot get into or out of themselves, and this is echoed by Lansbury (2012:1), who tells us that 'sitting babies up prematurely prevents them from rolling, twisting, scooting or doing much of anything else. When an infant is placed in this position before he is able to attain it independently, she usually cannot get out of it without falling, which does not encourage a sense of security or physical confidence'.

It is worth thinking about when we reflect on our own practices with babies in relation to the use of restrictive devices such as chairs for babies, bouncers and bumbos and even when introducing tummy time, as she would argue this is unnatural for a child if they cannot roll over when they choose: 'from approximately six months of age, when the infant could be able to try out a variety of movements, s/he is hardly given the opportunity to do so' (Pikler, 1979:6). We need to think carefully about the opportunities we afford to babies and how they may affect their development, giving them time and space to research their own movements. Many of us, myself included, have been guilty in the past of prematurely propping our babies up. What matters is that we educate ourselves and try to discover the best ways to promote healthy, natural development for our infants whilst maintaining trusting relationships. There is nothing wrong with tummy time for young children, but it should be done in such a way that is respectful of the child's capabilities.

Loris Malaguzzi (1920–1994)

We have seen so far that many of the theories feature key elements that are returning to our practice and our environments today. One such approach that embodies what it means to respect children and their strong, capable nature is that of the Reggio Emilia schools in Italy. The influence the Reggio Emilia pedagogy has had in recent years on early years provision is profound, with many leaders and practitioners flocking to the city each year to see their approach to learning and developing in young children. I'm sure it is on the wish list of many who have yet to go.

Loris Malaguzzi, the first director of Reggio's early services, developed the Reggio Emilia schools in Italy based on 'subjectivity, dialogue, connection and autonomy' as well as 'the understanding of problems through experiment, trial, error and testing, a pedagogy of listening' (Vecchi, 2010: xvi). This is perfect for young children who are learning about the world in this way. We often hear about Malaguzzi and the notion of a child having a hundred languages and as Edwards (2002) notes, children grow in competence to symbolically represent ideas and feelings through any of their hundreds of languages (expressive, communicative and cognitive). After 'rejecting Piaget's stage notions as too limiting, he drew a powerful image of the child, social from birth, full of intelligence, curiosity and wonder' (Edwards, 2002: 10) and set about creating a curriculum that 'has purposive progression but not scope and sequence' with a focus on relationships, meaningful documentation and the environment as the third teacher.

It is not new thinking that babies are capable human beings, and the well-known ideas of Malaguzzi (cited in Ebrahim, 2011: 121) seen worldwide in what are now known as Reggio-inspired settings suggest that children are not simply adults in the making but that they 'are strong, powerful, competent and have the ability to connect with adults and peers' (Dahlberg & Moss, 2005: 155). This way of viewing even the youngest children has been adopted by many early years practitioners as more research becomes available and the idea of the competent child is explored and embedded in practice. As Malaguzzi (1993: 10) states, 'our image of the child no longer considers them isolated and egocentric…instead…the child is rich in potential, strong, powerful, competent and most of all connected to adults and other children'. Within this idea of the 'rich' child as described above by Malaguzzi, 'learning is not an individual cognitive act' but is a 'cooperative and communicative activity'.

Putting the theories into practice

There are, as we have seen, many founding ideas based on what we know about human knowledge and child development. The way we view children, how we design our early years settings and the experiences that happen within them is based on these pioneering theorists, and their work underpins much of what we know about babies and their innate curiosities and needs.

Squirrels Family and Childcare Centre in Northamptonshire is a Curiosity Approach accredited nursery. They reflect on their influences:

We have an ethos based on the pedagogy and approach to learning through Steiner, Reggio and such like. The nursery is stripped back to basics and we have approximately 20% plastic maximum throughout the nursery and use real/natural materials throughout, creating awe and wonder as a stimulation and sensory experience. We also have scents through the rooms using a wax melt system and authentic ingredients to stimulate children's smell.

Squirrels Family & Childcare Centre

At Carlene's Cubbyhouse Family Day Care, Carlene takes elements of the Reggio philosophy and challenges us to think critically about what we do and how we do it with young children, particularly in response to the idea that the environment is the third teacher:

> The Third Teacher welcomes children in, makes them feel valued and important, makes them feel safe and invites them to play. Think about your setting; think about the very first impression that greets a child as they walk through the door, what are the sounds, smells and visual aspects that greet that child? Those impressions will set the scene for how a child responds to your environment and also set the scene for your day together! If a child is greeted with loud noises, overstimulation, and lots of bright, noisy toys how do you think they will react? If they are greeted with soft music, incense and areas to play that look interesting, but not overwhelming, do you think their reaction will be different? If a child feels welcome, they will feel safe. Children who feel safe can get on with play – and that means learning.

Both of the examples here reflect the importance of the environment in early years and creating an atmosphere that welcomes children and supports transitions as well as providing a space for exploration and curiosity. In all Reggio-inspired settings, the environment is viewed as the third teacher, and great care is taken to ensure children have a space where they have the freedom to explore a variety of interests and extend on them with meaningful resources carefully placed to ensure the best possible use.

It is not just children who benefit from this way of thinking. We spend the majority of our lives in our places of work, so it is important to reflect on these areas and make changes to ensure that we are calm and that our minds are free from clutter, ready to focus on the small humans we are lucky enough to spend our days with.

At Your Nursery Ltd, practitioners take a range of influences and weave them into all aspects of their practices with young children:

> Our ethos is based on Reggio Emilia but there is a large twist of other influences that make our setting very unique. We believe that children are capable learners and we constantly challenge them to encourage continued growth and development. Our planning is in the moment and we like to encourage children to have many new interests. Our baby room is designed with neutral colours in mind to prevent over stimulating young minds.

Whatever your influences and wherever your inspirations come from, it is vital that leaders are continually reflecting on what they offer and why. With new cohorts of children, the environment, activities and approaches may have to change, and it is important that this is recognised and not simply allowed to remain stagnant.

> Firstly, begin from the child's perspective. Get down to the children's height, crawl around and have a good look from their viewpoint. Take photos from the aspect of you as an adult and from the aspect of the child, so you can reflect on your set ups and compare the perspectives. Be aware that when you are creating the space, is it for you or is it for the children? Be prepared that the children may take the beautiful area that you created and take it in a completely different direction. (Carlene Cox-Newton)

The following case studies from CurioCity Childcare and Wally's Day Nursery help to demonstrate how various approaches and underpinning theories of learning and development have been embedded into all aspects of the setting, from the focus on developing the environment and the interactions that take place to the variety of resources that they provide.

CASE STUDY – CURIOCITY CHILDCARE

We do not have a permanent set up as such. Our rooms are forever changing and evolving to meet the needs and interests of children currently attending. Even though we are new, we've already changed so many things as we accept new children and look at ways to meet their needs better. However, we always seek approval and ideas from children as we want them to feel that they are in control of the spaces/rooms etc.

Our setting is inspired by Reggio Emilia and Scandinavian approaches. We concentrate massively on open ended resources, independence and full body, real life experiences.

Toys are not a necessity for us, instead we aim to repurpose/upcycle and reuse things from real life and our households. Babies in particular love real stuff, we therefore provide lots of pots, pans, remotes, car keys, boxes etc. We constantly work on training our staff so that they can look for opportunities, scaffold learning and be confident in risk assessing all activities as risk taking is something that we also promote.

We provide babies with sensory and taste safe provocations on a daily basis.

Babies also love our separate sensory room which is full of lights, sensory equipment, reflective resources etc as is our under 2s room. We tried to create a calm, neutral space inspired by nature around us but we welcome and encourage colours in our setting too.

After replacing much of the plastic in previous settings and seeing improvements in children's behaviour and learning it was clear that staff at CurioCity Childcare wanted a full refurbishment, switching from bright neon walls and run-down interiors to light, fresh airy playrooms. Being a relatively new setting, the staff are looking forward to seeing children's behaviour change for the better.

In this case study, we can see elements of the many theories discussed above, in particular the reflections on how staff wanted the setting to look and feel for the children. After seeing the impact in previous settings, staff made the commitment to change their environment in order to see the positive impact that a calm, neutral, well-resourced setting can have on the children's behaviour and learning.

CASE STUDY – WALLY'S DAY NURSERY

Over the course of writing this book, I have had the pleasure of several conversations with other managers of day nurseries and home-based providers from across the globe who have all provided images and annotations of their environments and some of the influences and underpinning theory that supports their practice. The following case study outlines the theory and underpinning knowledge that practitioners in the setting I manage use on a daily basis with our babies and some of the approaches to documentation and planning that we implement.

First and foremost, we work hard to ensure that babies at Wally's are valued and respected for the human beings they are. Even before parents register at our setting, we hold visits so that parents can come and meet the team and see the environment where their little one would play. I always ensure that I talk to the baby no matter their age or communicative ability, making eye contact and holding a 'conversation' waiting for them to respond. This tells them from the very beginning that they are important, and it is them who are the focus.

Much of our practice, like others who have contributed to this chapter, is based on the pioneers of early childhood. We are very reflective and as a team are highly qualified, so we have a lot of knowledge and experience of early years and have used this to shape our setting and constantly look for ways to improve every area of our provision.

We try to challenge the traditional ideas, focus on child-led practice and embed the idea that children need to have the opportunity to be autonomous in their environment, something which many staff can struggle with if they have had experience in less child-led environments previously, with more of a top down approach. We don't have templates, worksheets or daily prescribed activities.

We also try to challenge managerial stereotypes, particularly around their role. Traditionally managers are in offices not overseeing what happens in their nurseries. This is a fundamental difference in our setting as we try as much as possible to be available on the ground at all times. We know what is happening in each of our rooms and spend very little time sitting down. This means that we are able to support our staff in the moment and ensure that the children in our care get the best quality. We are also a nursery based on development rather than age, as we know and understand that children develop at different rates and it would be of no benefit to have designated 0-2, 2-3, 3+ rooms within our setting. With this way of working children can move when they are ready rather than when they have a birthday and respects entirely their individual development blueprint.

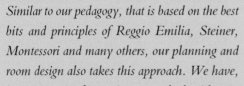

Similar to our pedagogy, that is based on the best bits and principles of Reggio Emilia, Steiner, Montessori and many others, our planning and room design also takes this approach. We have, in our years of experience, worked with many ways of planning and layout and understand that it should always reflect the cohort of babies in the room at any given

time and should be based on their interests, this is the same for planning, from old school formats and folders to paperless versions of in the moment planning. We have now taken what we know and like about all of these and found our own way to ensure we are planning mindfully, not producing too much paper but ensuring there is evidence of learning and progression for parents, inspectors and anyone who wants to see what we get up to at nursery.

We use elements of in the moment planning and the floor book approach with our babies and in fact all the children in the setting, as a way to ensure we are providing experiences that they are interested in, that will engage them and to ensure that they have a voice in their learning. We also create an online journal for each child ensuring parents have access and a scrapbook for the children to keep all of their best bits in.

Throughout this case study, it is clear that the care of young children is not a one-size-fits-all scenario, and what works for some does not necessarily work for others. For me, the focus on relationships is crucial to any successful childcare provision, and this is a view shared by many. Without a strong bond with not only the child but their family too, very little can be achieved together. This combined with a strong, dedicated team who are highly qualified means that our babies benefit not only from our years of experience but also from the example we set for them and our constant need to improve the experience they have within our setting.

TOP TIPS FOR REFLECTION

■ As a team, think about your individual influences. Each person should write down three bullet points that they believe to be crucial to baby care. Share these with the group.

- Are they the same?

- What are the differences?

- How are these interpreted in your practice?

■ Take time to reflect on the ethos and vison for the setting. Perhaps it needs rewording or updating to reflect your current families.

■ Stay strong – you don't have to go with the flow or do what others are doing. If you believe what you are doing is right and is in the best interests of the children you care for, stick with it. It might be that others are not ready for change.

The case studies that I have shared and the examples I have included in this book seek to demonstrate the wide-ranging theories that underpin the majority of practice in early years in the UK and around the world. In this chapter, we have explored some of these theories and considered how these are still relevant in today's early years climate. Many are linked through their approach to care, learning and experiences, and no matter where you work, each type of setting will take the elements that resonate with them and adapt them to their provision and community of children and families. What is important here is that the child remains at the centre of the decisions that are made to ensure that we give each child the best start for them, meeting them where they are and not where we think they should be at a given time.

4 Adult and baby relationships

'If a baby could tell us what she really likes from us, she would tell us that she would like three wishes: to feel safe, to feel loved and to be respected'. (Pennie Brownlee)

When thinking about the conditions that are needed for creativity to be fostered, the relationship between adult and baby is of paramount importance. In this chapter, we will explore the very beginning of human relationships with our babies, the important bonds they form in their first two years and how these are crucial to their later development. We will look at the different types of relationships that exist in the lives of our babies, from the strong bond they have with their families to the attachments they form with the practitioners who work with them in nurseries and why these relationships are important for their creative development.

Social from birth

In her book *Human Minds*, Margaret Donaldson puts forward the idea that 'neither our own abilities nor our preferences develop in isolation from the other human beings among whom we live and grow' (1992: 247). This statement alone provides evidence for the importance of others in the way we develop our sense of self and our thoughts and feelings. It also provides interesting thoughts on the idea that, without social context, 'abilities and preferences' would simply not develop. We all know the importance of building strong, purposeful relationships with others – people we can trust and who trust us and whom we care about. The relationships we build with other people form the basis of all other human connection, and this desire for social and emotional connection starts from the moment of conception and stays with us throughout our lives.

It is said that there are huge differences in the experiences that babies receive at home to those that are available in nurseries and home settings across the country, and, of course, there should be. They are fundamentally different in their purpose and the role that they have in a baby's life. The home is a place of security and love; it brings a sense of calm that no other place in the world can replicate. And whilst many settings are now striving to provide a 'home from home' environment, it can never take the place of a baby's home and the feelings that are derived within it. From the moment a family finds out they are expecting, a range of emotions flood the body, which are followed by a sequence of events triggered by the announcement that they are pregnant. In no other circumstance does this sequence of events exist; it is unique to each family, and everyone experiences it differently. It is here that the first bonds of parenthood begin. Even before birth, the bond a mother has with her child can be profound (but it must be noted this is not always the case). Most expectant mothers will 'talk' to their babies, and even in utero as they grow, babies will respond to noise by kicking.

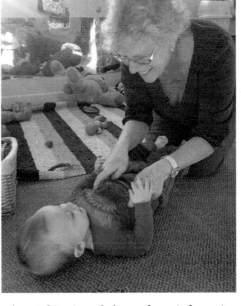

All babies are sensorimotor learners. When they are born, they have a well-developed sense of touch, which is why it is so important to ensure we have as much physical contact with our babies as possible. The majority of their senses, though, are concentrated in certain parts of their body, which is why there has been an increase in interest over the years in infant massage and baby yoga, and we can see these sessions slowly making their way into more and more baby rooms. As well as the benefits of physical contact, these special sessions provide crucial bonding time for parents and young babies and allow them to form attachments to special people.

Babies are social from birth and can appear very alert during their awake periods, when they are busy taking in a plethora of new information every minute, and we know they show a preference for human faces. Spending time with

babies and talking to them is the best way to support their understanding of the new world that they find themselves in. The first real sign of a social smile (from around the age of six weeks, although it can be later) is a special moment for parents, as it is at this point that babies are seen as interactive, something which can be especially important to older siblings who until this point have watched baby simply feed and sleep.

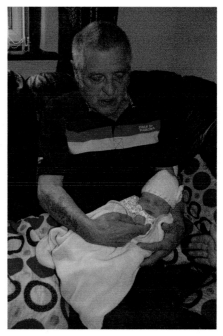

The majority of their lives are still feeding and sleeping, but this early social connection makes all the difference and is the beginning of a lifelong journey. Part of this journey that often happens within the first few weeks and months is the introduction to siblings and extended family members, many of whom may belong to the older generation. These intergenerational connections are deeply important to babies, and some of the bonds that are formed are much like that of a parent – unbreakable.

It has long been thought that babies are 'boring'; this is reflected in the lack of anthropological research on infants as 'they appear so much at the mercy of others that there does not appear to be any push and pull between individuals or between individual and society at large that makes for such interesting scholarly consideration' (Gottlieb, 2000: 124). As parents and early years practitioners working with babies, this is difficult to hear, and we are advocates for the fact that 'passivity is far from a complete description of a newborn's life....They (in many ways) demand to be accounted for' (Gottlieb, 2000: 124) and this continues for most of their early years.

Early communication

Babies also communicate in a range of ways despite the fact that they cannot speak, and this communication needs to be understood in order to meet the babies' needs. This is relevant for those in early years settings. As we get to know each baby individually, we know what each cry means and can tell the difference between them. This is a skill that takes real knowledge of each baby and their development and is something not all practitioners have. 'Crying is an irritant and people respond to it as an irritant, wanting to make it go away. Our goal should not be to stop crying, but to understand what the cry means and decide whether or not to intervene.

Allowing a child to cry requires more knowledge, time and energy than just picking up a child and patting her' (Gerber, cited in Gunning, 2016:1). This is hard for some practitioners to understand, particularly if they are new to the sector or are older and are of the mindset that babies just need a cuddle. There is nothing wrong with a well-placed cuddle, but with sensitive observation, knowledge of child development and a genuine care for the best interests of the babies we care for, we can connect on a deeper level with the babies in our care and find the reason for the crying rather than just getting it to stop.

TOP TIPS FOR BUILDING STRONG BONDS FROM BIRTH

■ Make eye contact.

■ Pull faces.

■ Sing or speak in a high-pitched tone (infant-directed speech).

■ Return babies' vocalisations.

Forming relationships with the whole family

Parents may not have as much underpinning knowledge about child development as those who have studied for years the complexities of brain development and developmental milestones of children in a particular age range, but they are their child's first educators and have a wealth of knowledge to share. Whilst there is no right or wrong way to bring up a child, each and every family will have their own views that can sometimes cause tension between families and providers. These can easily be overcome if strong, respectful relationships have been formed from the beginning with the family.

These relationships, which begin the moment parents visit a potential nursery or home educator, form the basis of what could potentially be years of care. It is a big step to entrust other human beings with the care of their child, and as managers and practitioners working with families, we have to understand that before we can begin to build any kind of relationship. 'It is important to respect this first bond with their parent or main carer and understand that it cannot be severed suddenly or pulled apart' (Gunning, 2016: 2). It is vital that transitions into any setting but in particular those with large numbers of children and staff are well thought out, planned and meet the needs not only of the baby but their parents too. Babies are driven by their innate desire for connection. Their body language, distinct cries depending on their needs at a given time and eye contact are ways that they seek to gain attention in those earliest weeks and months. For young babies in nursery, it can be hard to adjust to the different environment and the volume of people that somehow seem to exist all of a sudden. It is important that practitioners understand the emotional impact this can have and support solid, smooth transitions into nursery not only for the babies themselves but also for the parents, who may be finding the prospect of nursery care difficult particularly with complex emotions such as fear and guilt, which are often present in new parents returning to work.

The ideas of Maslow (1943) and his theory of human motivation, laid out in a 'pyramid shaped hierarchy of needs' (Abulof, 2017: 1), are influential in trying to understand and unpick what it means to be human and the inherent motivations we experience. Abulof (2017:508) eludes to the changing needs of society, suggesting that 'millennials have growing doubts about their capacity to fulfil the basic, material needs of the pyramid' and that increasingly society does not 'merely feel a need to belong, but to be needed – to gain a sense of self-worth'. This is important to the development of young children, particularly if we are trying to support creative independent thinking, as individuals who are finding it difficult to fulfil their own basic needs and have a desire to be needed are likely to be those parents whose children we see in early years unable to complete tasks independently or without reassurance, children who are not being given the opportunity to develop their autonomy and are risk averse for fear of failure. It is becoming an increasingly important part of our role as educators not only to build relationships with and care for the children in our settings but also to consider the family unit and the child's personal context and provide support and encouragement on a range of subjects. This can take its toll on practitioners, who are often left working against what they believe to be right in order to honour parents' requests and, in some cases, demands.

As we have seen, it is a huge decision to leave your baby somewhere unfamiliar to them, and there are questions and anxieties that must be addressed if trusting relationships are to be formed. It could be said that managers in early years settings have a strange role of almost selling their business to potential parents in the hope of securing what could be years of care for their child. Parents have often reported on visiting my setting that we are a friendly, down-to-earth, loving group of practitioners, and our children look very happy (which is always lovely to hear), but their experiences of other settings have often not been this way. In their study, Pungello and Kurtz-Costes (1999:32) determined that parents were more likely to choose childcare providers that are 'warm and loving, personable and experienced, reliable and trustworthy'. At such a critical time for the early years agenda and the current uncertainty that we face as a profession, of course we have businesses to run and a commitment to our staff; however, without our families, we would cease to exist entirely. It is important that, when offering visits to potential families, we take steps to ensure we start at the very beginning and build a rapport with parents and children, as this is often the first glimpse into what it is like to be a child at your setting.

The key person approach

In early childhood settings, the relationships that are formed play a vital role in the overall development of babies – not only in a creative sense but in all areas of learning. Without strong attachments to their caregivers, children cannot thrive. We know from working with babies that the most important thing, above almost all else, is the relationships that they form with those around them, primarily parents, as discussed above, but then, in the case of early years settings, those practitioners who work closely with them.

The ideal way for children to cope with the transition into an environment outside the home at such a young age is to ensure that they have one consistent familiar person with whom they can form an attachment. This attachment will not take the place of the parent but instead complement it to ensure that each child will have a smooth transition into a setting. In the UK, it is part of the early

years foundation stage statutory framework that all children in any group provision are given a key person. Underpinned by many aspects of attachment theory and now part of every nursery up and down the country, the key person approach to caring for young children has had a huge impact on the well-being of our children, ensuring that no matter how many adults and children they come into contact with, they know they have one special adult who is there to look after their well-being and make them feel safe.

There are many variations of children grouped by age, ability or in what some nurseries call 'family groups', and each setting will have its own ideas about how best to implement the approach based on their knowledge of the children and staff they have. The approach isn't without its difficulties, though, as Manning-Morton and Thorp (2003) suggest. They acknowledge these difficulties, which include practitioners struggling to form bonds with children for fear of getting too close or having their own emotional difficulties which mean they cannot fully commit to sensitive interaction. They go on to add that practitioners should have certain qualities in order to fulfil their role as key person. This is important because, often, practitioners can get caught up in what they believe the child needs or may overlook what is needed because they don't feel it is necessary. This brings us back to the idea of ensuring the babies' needs are always at the forefront. Through mindful observations, we can ensure we act always in their best interests.

The notion of professional love

Babies need love and affection to thrive. In the home environment, this is provided unconditionally by parents. However, early years practitioners, particularly those who work with the youngest children, will often report that they feel a bond with the babies they work with similar to what they may have with their own children. This has led to a strong debate over the controversial concept of professional love and brings into question the differences between care and love and the emotional state of mothers leaving their infants in order to return to work. David et al. (cited in Page, 2011:312) suggest that 'deep, sustaining and reciprocal relationships between adults and children are vital for children's holistic development', and whilst we know this to be true, it calls into question the type and quality of

the relationships that are formed with babies in our care. To suggest that 'caring in education is simply gentle smiles and warm hugs' (2011: 312) 'obscures the complexity and intellectual challenge of work with young children and is detrimental to the field' (Goldstein, 1998: 244).

Page (2011) identifies a need for parents and practitioners to engage in dialogue with regards to a need for love within a baby's learning, and Lynch (cited in Page, 2011:313) suggests that

'love labouring' at a 'mental level, involves holding the persons and their interests in mind, keeping them 'present' in mental planning and anticipating and prioritizing their needs and interests. Emotionally, it involves listening, affirming, supporting and challenging, as well as identifying with someone and supporting her or him emotionally at times of distress'.

From my own personal experience, I am glad to have found practitioners that appeared to 'love' both of my children. As a parent, I was not concerned that the love and bond I have with my own children would diminish, as can be a concern for some mothers. I also had trust in the fantastic practitioners I left my babies with and knew that it would remain at all times a 'professional' version of love as discussed above, one that puts my baby's needs first and keeps their interests and learning at the forefront. This resulted in loving, trusting relationships being formed with both of my children and their key people. My daughter, who is seven at the time of writing, still frequently visits and talks of her time in the baby room, and as my son (now three and a half) moves through the nursery, I am certain that these early attachments outside our family supported and encouraged him into becoming the confident, curious little boy he is.

It is not within the remit of this book to find evidence for or against the concept of professional love and argue one way or another. However, it is important to note that showing our babies 'love' and affection with eye contact, physical contact and conversation undoubtedly causes increased attachment, makes babies feel valued and helps to regulate their mood through continued exposure to such actions. Of the points that have been raised by Lynch (2007) in terms of what professional love may entail, I think it is absolutely a possibility that what practitioners do is 'love' the babies in their care as they are required on a daily basis to plan for, support, listen to, keep a mental note of evolving interests and prioritize the needs of the babies in their rooms.

Laura Brothwell from Stone Hen Childcare incorporates these ideas into her provision for babies too. She believes, along with many practitioners, that developing secure bonds and relationships has to be the key foundation for any form of creative learning to take place.

REFLECTION

- What do you think about the notion of 'professional love'? Is it something that you identify with, or do you think it is inappropriate in early years?

- Write down some of the differences that exist between 'care' and 'love' and discuss these with your staff team.

The importance of interaction

> Every child deserves a champion; an adult who will never give up on them, who understands the power of connection and insists that they become the best they can possibly be. (Rita F. Pierson)

Every time we interact with babies, we are sending a message. It is important that we understand the messages we are sending to our babies and are clear about how and what we are communicating. Every time a baby is spoken to, they are given a clear message about what it means for them, what they mean and their value to those around them. What they hear daily becomes their inner voice. The voice of disappointment or encouragement is dependent on the words they hear each day in their early years. Interaction with others has long been recognised as the foundation to all subsequent learning, and it is these interactions that play such a pivotal role in the development of young children's agentic behaviour, something which provides the foundation for creative thinking.

MacNaughton and Williams (cited in Rose & Rogers, 2012: 7) have shown that 'in a typical day early year's practitioners might have over a thousand interpersonal interactions with children', giving ample opportunity to support and encourage them in a way that promotes their development in all areas and gives them a voice. These 'interpersonal interactions' and the environment in which they happen (which we look at in chapter 5) should be taken together. As Kress indicates, 'what the childish eye falls on…exceeds in entirely unpredictable ways the conventionalised expectations of any adult' (1997: 122). This suggests that the materials that children find interesting and want to use are often unique to them and that without resources at a somewhat accessible level, children have no other option but to remain within the realms of what the adult intends or suggests. This is particularly relevant for babies, as many settings do not offer entirely accessible resources for young children, so it is important that the adults are sensitive to the needs and interests of the babies they care for in order to notice their fascinations and act on them accordingly, either by letting them play out independently (therefore allowing free choice and autonomy for the baby) or facilitating an invitation to investigate further. By providing resources and activities that are solely adult directed or initiated, an overreliance on the adult can develop. Even more damaging, completely adult-directed activities close off vital opportunities to develop creativity because the baby only has access to what the adult chooses or lays out for them.

One setting that strikes this balance is Bright Stars Nursery. Although their art materials are not accessible at all times, other resources are placed at child height to encourage independence and decision making.

Staff provide a range of exciting and thought-provoking invitations to learning for their youngest children, allowing them the freedom to choose how they use the resources. Their play

dough station houses a range of natural loose parts to encourage children to make permanent structures and allows young children the chance to create on their terms using their own ideas, not predesigned laminated mats or under adult instruction.

The example from Bright Stars Nursery and no doubt many other settings that work in this way across the country shows that when practitioners really care about the babies they look after and provide beautiful, stimulating environments that allow them the opportunity to think for themselves, it sends the children an important message: that they are capable and that their ideas are worthwhile and valued.

Another key role of the practitioner in supporting a child is Bruner's idea of 'scaffolding' (Duffy, 2006: 119). This happens when practitioners take what the children are saying or in the case of babies what they are doing and extend it, providing new information so that the children can 'attach it to existing knowledge' (Duffy, 2006: 120). This is crucial because without this, children would not be able to further develop their thoughts or creative processes; they would be unable to build on what they already know, and therefore the potential for further learning is greatly decreased. Duffy argues that 'creativity and imagination need stimulation' (2006: 146). Even very young babies need engaging, well-placed adult interactions and time together to build on their developing idea of the world and those in it. Failure to 'scaffold' what the child already knows would lead to the lack of 'stimulation' that Duffy suggests, creating a deficit in what is necessary to promote creativity.

The babies at Nina's Nursery High Lane are encouraged to explore their invitations to play alongside adults who are present and engaging and ready to scaffold their learning when necessary. We can see in these images that the children were offered different objects to investigate, including a herb plant. One baby was unsure but found comfort in Katie, one of the practitioners at the

setting. After Katie had demonstrated smelling and touching the herb, it instilled confidence in the baby, who then came back to explore the herb a second time, this time touching part of the plant without sitting directly with the practitioner. Another baby was keen to touch the plant and brought it closer to Katie's face after they had seen her smelling the herb prior to their engagement.

When working with babies, it is vital that we understand that all of our interactions mean something. We have already discussed how the way we communicate sends a message and how our body language often speaks volumes to those around us. This doesn't mean that we have to be interacting 100 per cent of the time; sometimes sitting back and observing children takes as much skill as the engagement itself, particularly for staff who think it means they aren't doing anything. Instead, what it means is that you are carefully watching and remaining present and attentive. Babies need time to explore independently, knowing they are in the presence of a safe adult who, when the time comes, is ready to respectfully join in, scaffold appropriately and share in their joy.

Expectation

It is important that the adults around babies have realistic expectations of them, and the only way to do this is to tune in to what is known about child development and simple biology. Learning alongside babies through the relationships that have been built ensures that our expectation levels remain in tune with what is achievable at a given moment. This is something important to note in terms of new practitioners to the sector and their understanding of what young children are capable of. Early childhood qualifications in the UK are still predominantly based on a Piagetian framework of child development; therefore, some of the more recent developments are not included in the training that is available. This is not the student's fault, and many who are passionate about early years will quickly learn that there is increasing evidence to suggest that babies are extremely capable and are not, as some have considered in the past, simply adults in the making. Nutbrown (1996: 36) uses Donaldson's notion of the knowledgeable child as she describes how adults can sometimes (often unintentionally) have a tendency to 'look out on the world from one's own position'. This is apparent in a study conducted by Recchia and Dvorakova (2012: 195), who found that practitioners' expectations change depending on the age of the children that they work with. This is particularly important in regard to infants, as they have historically been viewed as 'passive recipients'. Thankfully this is no longer the case, and those working with babies have the knowledge and skills to understand what they can do and how to support them effectively.

Expectations and boundaries are closely linked and often come hand in hand when talking about the mutual respect we aim to foster with children. If a child grows up in an environment of pleasing adults and following rules, they learn very quickly that they must follow instructions and do exactly as they are told. These ideals, when enforced in the wrong way, can lead a child to feel that they are unable to experiment the way they would choose to, effectively putting aside their innate creativity in favour of adult expectations. (If you haven't read the poem 'The Little Boy' by Helen E. Buckley, it is definitely worth a read.)

This is detrimental to the adult–child relationship. It is well known that all children thrive on boundaries and knowing what is expected of them, so I am not saying that we have to forget this entirely and let children do what they want all the time, but it is crucial that we strike the balance between our expectations of young children, what they are physically and emotionally capable of at any given stage in their development and allowing them the freedom to choose how and what they want to engage with. As adults, we need to trust that our children will try new things and take safe risks. Again, I am not saying that we should just let our babies crawl freely across roads or wander independently around busy streets – there is always a level of supervision in place and so there should be; however, when babies are well supervised and a responsive adult is present to keep them safe, they should be able to experiment with different ways of doing things without direct adult interference, thus instilling in the child a sense of wonder, developing creativity and using skills that they will continue to build on.

I once visited a museum, and as my own children were playing, I watched a family with their young daughter. I'd say she was a year old, perhaps a little older, crawling confidently and wearing a lovely pair of shiny red shoes. Holding the hand of her grandmother, she was able to walk, if a little unsteadily, but she smiled proudly before letting go and crawling away. There was a slope in the centre of the play area not more than four inches off the ground at the bottom, and the little girl, not interested in the array of cars, crawled over and pulled up to stand at the slope. Her mother immediately instructed her grandmother to get her as 'she may hurt herself'. I watched as she was taken from where she was stood and placed, sitting, in another area. She crawled three more times over to the slope and was removed three more times before the family packed their things, put the little girl back in her pram and walked away. I watched as she was wheeled away, and in the moments before I turned my attention back to my children (now busy playing with their dad), I thought of the message that little girl had received: we don't trust you; you are not as able as you think; and we have to stop you from finding out independently about space, height, texture and strength to keep you safe.

REFLECTION

- Think about the little girl in the museum. Discuss as a group what messages this little girl unconsciously received and what this might mean.

- Reflect on what you know about the Pikler approach from chapter 3 – what might Emmi Pikler have said?

The example above can also be applied to the early years in relation to the importance of support from a creative adult and the impact when that support is not in place. In terms of boundaries and expectations, there is a fine balance between putting these things in place and supporting young children to manage safe risks. The same can be said about creative endeavours. As with the example in the museum, if the little girl were left with no adult support, she may indeed have been hurt, but if her caregivers had chosen to sit close by and talk to her throughout her attempts at standing independently, the learning and opportunities for engagement would have greatly increased.

In terms of our children's creative development, if we were to allow children 'complete freedom with no adult support, the result is likely to be unplanned chaos, with little regard to the choice of resources, mess, wastage and the learning is likely to be minimal' (Compton et al, 2010: 18), particularly when we think about babies. However, with the right level of engagement, active participation and observational periods from sensitive practitioners, 'children with different creative abilities and potentials can be supported and each process and product is explicitly valued and intrinsic motivation is encouraged' (Compton et al, 2010: 18). This allows all children to get involved if they choose and allows the opportunity for each child to explore at their own pace, something which is important to young children in understanding that they are valued and important.

Babies are the perfect explorers; they do not need our help. What they need is the trust of a familiar adult and the opportunity to exercise their autonomy – only then will they achieve what they are truly capable of at a time when they are ready.

We have seen throughout this chapter the important role that relationships play in shaping the way young children view their world. Babies need strong bonds with family members and extended family in order to develop a sense of self and where they fit in; once at nursery, babies need a familiar adult who will advocate for them and practitioners who will provide, on a daily basis, a sensory-rich environment and stimulating activities whilst maintaining the relationships they have built with babies and their families.

5 Developing a creative baby room environment

Introduction

What is it that babies need in their earliest months and years in order to develop the skills and competencies essential for future creative thinking? We know from the previous chapter about the importance of the adult role, especially for babies, and we have established a definition of creativity that seems to value the skills and thought processes required. In this chapter, we will look in depth at the environment, the practical aspects that need to be considered and the differences that exist between rooms for babies and those for older children. We will explore the importance of providing an environment that encourages the development of creativity and how it is subsequently explored by the babies who use it and some of the disparities between what we think a baby room should look like in theory or what we would like it to look like (usually based on what we have been inspired by on various social media platforms) and the practicalities involved in setting up, designing and using a baby room.

Common themes

We have already explored some of the reasons why the development of creativity is important and how we can support it in our practice, so what about where these interactions take place and to what extent the spaces we provide promote or discourage children from expressing their creative ideas? Most practitioners will have come across several common themes that are reflected in most baby room environments regardless of the ethos or values in the setting. These often include the desire for soft furnishings, having places for babies to sit and reflect and the placement of mirrors, which often feature heavily in baby rooms due to the number of benefits of their reflective properties and differing perspectives that they offer to young babies.

> Mirrors and reflective surfaces are a great way to promote self-awareness, focus and explore the wonderful things a face can do. Mirrors help babies to observe the world from new perspectives both vertically and horizontally. Activities like this provide our little ones with

the opportunity to express themselves freely and to get creative with sounds and movements in those early months. (Laura Brothwell)

Many reading this who work in baby rooms already will have their own ideas about what a baby room should look like, both in theory and in practice, based primarily on their own experiences and the settings they have encountered. Whilst many settings are similar in their approach to designing spaces for young babies, often it is the practice that happens within them that sets them apart.

Why are baby rooms different?

Baby rooms have a unique responsibility in providing some of the very first relationships outside of the family unit. It is baby room staff who have the unique role of building relationships not only with the babies they care for but with their parents too, who come to choose childcare for a variety of reasons and may be feeling a range of emotions about parting from their children for the first time for even a small portion (or for some, a large majority) of their week. For this reason, there is a huge responsibility on the shoulders of those who work in baby rooms to provide high-quality care and experiences for the youngest children in early years provision, many of whom will be experiencing this type of environment for the first time.

For many reasons, baby rooms are fundamentally different in the way they are set up and organised compared to other rooms in nurseries that are designed for older children. When we think about setting up rooms for babies, the chances are that we will all have come across a handful of different layouts, colour schemes, resources and space differences. These are based, more often than not, on a setting's knowledge of the founding theories within early childhood alongside their own ideas about what babies need and their understanding of good-quality environments. These will be unique to each setting, and as those who have worked in different types of provision will know, no two baby room spaces are the same and neither should they be. Each one should reflect the community it serves and the babies who use it and attempting to produce a carbon copy of an image we like is doing the babies we care for a disservice. This is the difficulty in marrying both the idea of what the environment should look like or what we want it to look like and creating it in practice.

We know that babies are all different, with different interests and development pathways, therefore what works in one setting may not work in others, and it would be naïve to think that reproducing an environment will create the same outcome. Instead, the focus should always be on the needs of the babies in your particular setting, their interests and their fascinations. By all means use images for inspiration but we must remain mindful of

our own strengths and limitations, holding on to what our babies need and their schematic play preferences and ensuring that we understand fully the reasons for our choices before changing the environment.

The emotional environment

The emotional environment that we create for babies is perhaps more important than any physical space we can design, and this was explored previously in chapter 4. Elizabeth Jarman, founder of the Communication Friendly Spaces approach, believes that 'the emotional climate is a priority when reviewing your learning environments. Creating homely, personalised places that feel familiar for your children alongside consistent, knowledgeable, responsive carers makes all the difference' (Jarman, 2019). In her book *Re-thinking Learning Environments for Children and Families* (2013), she points out that 'the quality of children's learning environments has not always been enough of a priority' but that this is gradually changing with more and more professionals taking on board the idea that 'the environment you offer can set the scene for meaningful learning and connection to take place' (2013: 5).

Once we are sure that we have created the right emotional environment for our babies through the use of professional discussions, ongoing professional development and valuable audit toolkits, we can then begin to look at our physical environment and what we need to have in place to ensure that we are truly embedding the ethos and values of the setting as well as creating an environment that is conducive to creative thinking with babies and young children who feel secure in their surroundings.

TOP TIPS FOR CREATING THE RIGHT EMOTIONAL ENVIRONMENT

■ Reflect on your settling-in policy for young babies and revise if needed.

■ Ensure all babies have a peg to hang their belongings.

■ Introduce chatterboxes for babies on entry (more on this in part 2).

■ Ask parents to provide photographs to display in the setting.

■ Display images of the children at their height so they have positive images of themselves. This will help them to feel a sense of value and belonging.

■ Provide commentaries for babies when you move around the room rather than simply getting up and walking away. This will instil a sense of trust.

Provision for mealtimes

The importance of getting the emotional environment right for babies should be high on the agenda for leaders in early years settings, and we have already seen how difficult it can be to design environments for babies that ensure staff maintain high standards of care as well as provide ample opportunities for babies to engage with the world around them. They must also consider the routines of each baby and how these can be facilitated to provide continuity of care and ensure that each baby's needs are met at the right time, and the provision they have in place must support this. If a child's needs are not met, it can have a detrimental effect on their emotional well-being, so it is important that we explore the impact this can have on the environment.

The age of the children in the room (most baby rooms in the UK take children from three months until their second birthday, whilst some in larger premises are able to separate their oldest babies from approximately eighteen months) will determine the type of provision that is needed for more practical aspects of the baby room, such as mealtimes, in terms of the equipment and furniture. Younger babies can easily be fed in highchairs, whilst older babies may need a table and low chair to support them as they begin to feed independently. There are a range of highchairs and tables available on the market that cater for the variety of room sizes and storage solutions, something which is important to consider when deciding whether they will stay out in the play space permanently or whether they can be stored away to save space. Only those working in the setting can determine what their particular children need, what developmental stage they are at and how best to cater for them. Whilst these decisions should be based on sound knowledge of child development, there are still occasions where things are done a certain way because 'that's how we do it' or 'the manager says we have to do it that way'.

Mealtimes are social occasions and should always be treated as such. Regardless of the physical equipment involved, babies and adults should enjoy mealtimes together as an exploratory stage in their development with lots of opportunity for creative discovery. But very often in settings, staff feel under pressure at these pivotal times of the day to adopt a conveyor belt of feeding and sleeping, which is extremely stressful for all involved.

This returns to the practical everyday side of running a baby room, ensuring that all the babies are fed and possibly also asleep to facilitate lunch times for staff or other 'jobs' that must be done. Skilled practitioners who appreciate the importance of a calm and purposeful mealtime routine need to challenge the ideas of others in order to get the best for the children they work with. Staff rotas should be altered to allow enough time for children to be fed in a way that promotes independence, builds and maintains important relationships and allows the baby to explore and enjoy mealtimes rather than being rushed through it to reach an end goal.

Babies should be seated appropriately in small groups to encourage communication and language between them and a familiar adult. Providing a commentary to very young babies will support their growing vocabulary, and research has shown the benefit that we all know talking to young children has. In the way that a good bedtime routine improves the likelihood of a smooth transition to sleep, the same can be said for mealtimes. If babies feel the tension build around this time of the day and see staff busying themselves with preparatory jobs, the transition and enjoyment around food can quickly be lost. It is vital that staff acknowledge this and organise their mealtimes flexibly around the needs of the babies to ensure that mealtimes remain calm and unhurried.

REFLECTING ON MEALTIMES

Consider with your team:

■ What do mealtimes look like in your setting?

■ Are babies given enough time to enjoy their meals/snacks with a familiar adult?

■ Are young children sitting together so that they can enjoy the social aspect that should accompany mealtime?

Think about your discussion; could anything be done differently to improve on this important time?

Physical space

First and foremost, it is important to remember that the physical space we have to work in plays a crucial role in how we design spaces for babies. Babies need room to move, and spaces with lots of furniture will inevitably limit a baby's range of free exploration, whatever capacity this comes in. Some settings worry that with not enough furniture, the room will look bland and perhaps even empty, but it is necessary to provide a large enough space for babies to play, move and discover what they can do within their environment, and spaces can easily avoid looking empty with a few well-placed rugs and small items to discover. Whether home based or in a purpose-built nursery where specific spaces have been designed to encourage and support creative thinking, each setting must be taken individually to 'maximise its potential for creativity and imagination' (Duffy, 2006:133). Whether you are working in a large space, small space, with or without a table, lots of floor space or hardly any, remembering to be mindful of the opportunities this provides and maximising the potential of your space when thinking about how to set it for babies and young children is vital.

The furniture we choose can define and create spaces but also has the potential to make or break a room and its overall effectiveness depending on how it is used. Depending on the individual setting, almost all baby rooms require furniture for practical day-to-day care routines, such as nappy-changing facilities and places to store care items (such as blankets or bedding) as well as a range of well-thought-out furniture to create spaces and nooks for babies, areas to play and areas to sleep and eat (although these may be elsewhere in settings that have additional rooms).

Often, before we think about the kinds of resources or play experiences we want to be able to provide for babies, we ask, where will they sleep? Where will they eat? Do we need a sleep room or milk kitchen? All very important questions to consider, but something which is unique only to baby rooms. Of course, babies sleep during the day, which means that consideration has to be given to where that will happen. When they are not eating or sleeping, babies also need room to move and explore freely on their own terms while they are gaining confidence in a range of physical skills that will eventually mean they can crawl or walk independently. Almost all other rooms are designed first and foremost for children who have already mastered this skill, meaning that they almost never have to consider nonmobile children or those who are unsteady on their feet. We know that when babies are well fed and rested and feel secure in their environment, their brains work more effectively, constantly making connections and exploring the world around them, which is why it is so important to get it right.

One setting that has designed their space to reflect the needs of the children and their ethos whilst providing a range of experiences for their youngest children is Your Nursery Ltd:

> Our baby room was designed to incite interest and exploration, there are lots of natural items that encourage babies to learn through their senses with wooden pegs, curtain rings, metal bowls, large pebbles, pinecones and an array of treasure baskets. We have a large wooden sandpit that babies can climb into and immerse themselves

in the sand. We also have a variety of sensory lights, bubble tubes and different sensory toys to develop learning through their senses. We often have the projector set up projecting a variety of videos onto the back wall, from an aquarium to bats, birds and other videos of nature, this is great for developing language and eye hand coordination as they follow the videos with their hands. We have a large circular

garden arch tipped onto its side this allows early walkers to develop their walking and balancing skills and there is a fenced off area that allows smaller non mobile children to sit in safety without being knocked over by the more mobile children. A small home corner allows the older age range to carry out pretend play and a door opens straight into the garden allowing for free flow play.

In this example, we can see that practitioners have thought about what they want to offer the children and the benefits each area will have – for example, the ability to be immersed in the sand pit or how nonmobile babies can remain safe in a fenced-off area of the environment.

Many settings throughout the UK are revisiting the work of some of the most renowned early years educators for inspiration and guidance when it comes to the environments and opportunities that they offer for babies and young children.

Reflections Nursery and Small School in Worthing draws inspiration for their environments

from the infant-toddler centres and the preschools of Reggio Emilia, where the environment is viewed as the third teacher, and they place a significant emphasis on materials for children's exploration:

This room is for children aged 3 months to 1 year – we have a separate sleep room.

In the image with the projection on the wall we hitched a camera to our fish tank at child-height in the baby room and projected it large on the wall for children to explore in scale. We juxtaposed feathers with this image for fun for the babies.

Here are some images of our older baby environments too (for children aged 1–2 years). As you can see, one room was given over as an exploration of bubble wrap – but the materials in the rooms change frequently, it has also been used as an exploration of cardboard. (Martin Pace, director of Reflections Nursery and Small School)

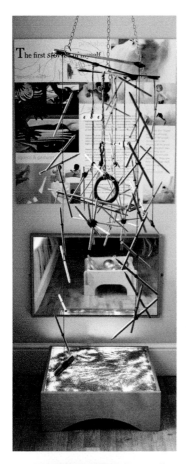

Providing a changing environment and a variety of new experiences for babies and young children to explore ensures that babies always have the opportunity to discover new and exciting ways to interact with the world and learn using all of their senses.

Another setting that has been inspired to think about their environment and the way they offer opportunities to the children in their care is Nina's Nursery High Lane.

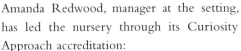

Amanda Redwood, manager at the setting, has led the nursery through its Curiosity Approach accreditation:

> This is where our influence originates following different ideas pulled from pioneers such as Steiner, Montessori and Reggio Emilia as well as pedagogues like Te Whariki. Here are some photos of our baby room environment and invitations to play, we incorporate natural, real resources for the babies to explore. The loose parts provided offer exploratory open-ended opportunities to play that provide new stimulus that otherwise may not be available to babies.

ENVIRONMENT REFLECTION

Ask yourself the following questions. (These can be used as a starting point for discussion.)

■ How often do you review your environment?

■ Who makes the decisions about how the environment should look and why?

■ What are your environment influences, and who does this benefit?

Space

Following on from the important idea that we cannot just re-create what someone else has done successfully and hope to achieve the same outcome, we must examine the implications of working in a baby room and the practical environment when caring for such young children. The importance of space is set out in the early years foundation stage statutory framework for providers to ensure they have adequate floor space for children in the three most typical age bands, and this has remained unchanged since its introduction in 2012. Babies receive the most space per child at 3.5m^2 with toddlers between the ages of two and three years old receiving a minimum of 2.5m^2 per child. That being said, despite being given the most space of all the age groups, it is often baby rooms that are the most challenging to arrange in terms of layout for the above-mentioned reasons.

Leaders in toddler rooms or preschools often don't feel the same pressure to think carefully about where the children will sleep, just that they should provide cosy spaces for relaxation if they need to. They have no need for a range of seating arrangements or the different types of chairs that will be needed for feeding, something which is often constant in the minds of those working in baby rooms. As children get older and move on to other rooms within a setting, their needs change, and as they develop fundamental skills such as walking, running and feeding themselves, it becomes much easier to focus on experiences whilst supporting their independence as their routines become more predictable, and around the age of two, usually follow a similar pattern to others the same age. This brings us back to the idea that baby rooms are fundamentally different in the way they are set up and the daily thought processes of those looking after such young children as they differ greatly from any other age group.

ENVIRONMENT REFLECTION

Take a moment to think about your current baby room. Sit or lie on the floor and look around from a child's perspective.

■ What can you see? Table legs, highchair legs, cots?

■ Do babies have space to move – stretching their arms and legs freely or rolling around?

The importance of colour

Colour plays an important role in the overall aesthetic of a space, it can also impact an individual's mood, emotional wellbeing, learning and behaviour. (Hellyn & Bennet, 2017: 21).

If you are already working in a baby room, the chances are that the colour of the walls is not something that you would have had a say in. Historically, baby room floors were covered with mats and play gyms featuring all of the colours of the rainbow, many plastic resources were a firm favourite on shelves and nursery walls were adorned with bright and highly stimulating colours and characters, thought to excite the children and make them feel welcomed by seeing familiar pictures on the walls. There is now a growing body of evidence that suggests this may not be the case and, in fact, that such wall spaces and displays are working against what those in baby rooms are trying to create: a calm, settling, welcoming environment where children feel at ease enough to explore their surroundings. In order to demonstrate this, it is helpful to think of our own homes and the way we choose to decorate particularly our living spaces in order to feel calm and relaxed after a busy day. Many would not choose to use bright rainbow colours to decorate their homes, so why do so many insist on this type of décor for our babies? Are they not deserving of a space that ignites curiosity and a feeling of serenity and a place where they can feel at peace in order to thrive?

This is not to be confused with the idea that all colour should be removed from baby room environments, simply that it should be used purposefully in terms of display to effectively showcase the children's learning and that resources should be thoughtfully placed to enhance the experience of the children, not overwhelm them. As Elizabeth Jarman (2013:92) suggests, 'it's about using colour in an informed, manageable way' and seeing the impact it can have on children's learning behaviours. It doesn't have to be expensive to remedy bright colours and cluttered spaces either. If you have made the decision to calm down your environment, stripping the display boards and opting for pastel tones or natural fabrics is a great way to start, and the difference is often striking.

When Bianca Johnson started her first nursery in 2017, she knew she wanted something to make her stand out from other types of provision in the local area. Having always worked in brightly decorated nurseries, she was determined to create something different:

I have knowledge of the Reggio Emilia Infant Schools and Montessori so this inspired me. I also wanted to enable my staff to have more time with the children so attended planning in the moment training in partnership with another setting. When I had the opportunity to visit their setting was very natural and that was it, when I saw the setting I knew that is what I wanted. We now follow the Curiosity Approach and we are on our journey to be accredited under this approach using natural and authentic resources.

Putting the children at the forefront and displaying pictures and paintings that are valuable to them on neutral tones makes the children's effort stand

out and shows that they are an integral part of the setting community. Often managers will have an action plan in place as big environment changes do not happen overnight and often require budgeting for. Perhaps organise a discussion with your staff team or colleagues to determine any areas for improvement that could be added to the action plan. Neutral rugs and cushions can help to take away some of the brightness of the carpets or historic vinyl and calm down a space. As mentioned previously, impact is important, and for those working with babies it is important to get it right. Even those who think they have their environment right should consider what can be improved. As cohorts of children move on and new children start, different behaviours and interests are apparent, and our environment must reflect those changes.

Lighting

Lighting also has a huge impact on the overall look and feel of an environment and the way it makes people feel. Lots of settings have no say over the lighting arrangements in their buildings (including my own), but softening them, especially in baby rooms, is seen as essential now to ensure that babies are calm and focussed rather than distracted by big open spaces and bright lights. Natural light is, of course, preferred, but where this isn't possible cosy spaces and lamps or other soft lighting arrangements can be made. Practitioners at Bright Stars Nursery make every effort to ensure their spaces for children are calm and neutral and incite wonder and curiosity with the twinkle of fairy lights.

ENVIRONMENT REFLECTION

Engaging in regular professional discussions with your team allows staff to broaden their own knowledge and see things from others' perspectives and provides practitioners the opportunity to talk about aspects of the environment that are working well or areas that may need improvement.

TOP TIPS FOR YOUR PHYSICAL ENVIRONMENT

■ Consider small nooks for babies to retreat to when they need some time alone. These can be created with fabric or cots turned on their sides or small structures if you have them.

■ Ensure all furniture serves a purpose and sell or recycle anything that you don't need.

■ Be mindful of the environment from a child's-eye view (table legs, highchairs, cots).

■ High ceilings can be brought down with fabrics, and soft lighting can be achieved with fairy lights, lamps or wall-mounted soft lights.

(continued)

- Try using hessian or a neutral fabric on display boards so as not to detract from the children's artwork.

- Hard floors can be softened with rugs, and harsh, brightly coloured flooring can be quickly calmed down with carpet offcuts or rugs.

- Ask parents for donations of fabrics or curtains to further soften rooms.

- Use colour mindfully, perhaps in colour spaces or themed areas.

- Use the furniture you have creatively to make nooks, corners or cosy dens if you don't have these in your room design.

The role of reflective practice in the environment

It is key that practitioners remain attuned to the needs of the group and continue to work to improve when particular aspects of the physical environment are no longer working to encourage independent, creative, free expression. Home-based provisions have a unique opportunity to be one of the most reflective types of provision (something which can be difficult to achieve in larger, group settings with a managerial structure and lots of staff working in each room). Being solely responsible for your environment and how and what you provide for babies does inevitably have its advantages, such as the ability to reflect on the day or a given week and change the environment readily and without hesitation.

Laura Brothwell from Stone Hen Childcare is a home-based provider who is constantly reflecting on her environment to ensure it meets the needs of the children and their fascinations.

She says, 'Our environment isn't switched at term time or monthly, we ensure that the provision meets the individual needs of our babies, resulting in an ever changing and adaptive environment following the babies holistic development and next steps'.

Any good-quality group provision should allow this kind of reflective practice, but many, even if they *are* reflecting on their environment and potential ways to improve it, are stopped in their tracks by colleagues, managers or other outside agencies who may have other ideas or see potential problems. This is something that we will all have had experience with at some time in our career. It is a good idea to get input from different sources, and professional discussions are invaluable to improving our own knowledge.

It is crucial, however, that any changes taking place are based on a clear vision for good practice rather than ideas of what should be provided, what might look 'nice' because someone else has done it already or what has been offered to children in the past. Furthermore, reflection in early years settings is a crucial element of self-evaluation and should be valued by all practitioners and management structures. The angle that staff take in this process will depend largely on their role in the setting and their own observations of the room itself and how the children behave within it. Whether management, key person or room leader, it is important for staff well-being as well as the experience of the children that regardless of role, these differences in professional opinion are  discussed and valued and, most importantly, that all those involved have the same shared vision.

Particularly relevant to this is the notion that in many early childhood settings, it is still the perceived child that is the focus, that is, the child we think we know, rather than who they really are. This is illustrated by Dahlberg et al. (2013: 46), who suggest that 'we have choices to make about who we think the child is and these choices have enormous significance....They determine the institutions we provide for children'. This is apparent in the aforementioned example as those working directly with the children will have a different perception of the children that they work with and what they might need than those in management roles not necessarily working with the children on a daily basis or those from regulatory bodies that view the setting in a snapshot manner, representing only a sample of the day. It is important therefore that when reflecting on environments for children there is a clear rationale in place and an understanding that, whilst it remains of critical importance to listen and take on board suggestions from others, ultimately we must ensure a 'child-centred' (Dahlberg et al., 2013: 46) approach in early childhood that reflects our own community of children and families and their needs rather than doing something simply because it is expected or because it has always been that way.

Finding your why

When looking through the amazing amount of imagery and inspiration that is available online, on social media and in books, it is easy to lose sight of why practitioners do what they do in their own settings, wanting to redesign and develop areas or go on a spending spree to create a replica of something that has inspired them. It is largely down to the individual setting, the needs of the children, the creative adults that support the children and the underfunding and budget constraints that affect all nurseries as to how they manage their environment, but it is vitally important to remember that your setting is unique.

It is unique to its families and children and those who work within it. All early years provision, regardless of its size, its premises or its budget, should have a clear rationale for the type of childcare and experience that they want to provide and a vision for the environment and learning that they want to happen within it. It is this that drives forward improvement and good practice and provides the opportunity to regularly reflect on what we want to achieve and how.

It is not my intention to advocate for a particular theory or style of baby room, only to provide evidence of the options that are available and inspiration for those who may be just starting out in their journey either as nursery practitioners, those hoping to open their own settings that may include a baby room or those who are looking to revamp their current set-up. I believe that if those who are working with the youngest children know why they are doing something and can provide clear evidence of the impact and benefit it will have to the young children they care for, then it really is an open opportunity to explore our own thoughts, values and beliefs and then embed them into practice.

6 Resourcing for a creative baby room

In this chapter we will explore what it means to select resources that will encourage creative thinking. In recent years, there has been a return to thinking about the types of resources that are best for babies to allow them to develop at their own pace, with objects that incite their innate creativity and where they are free to explore and experience the world. We will revisit some of the pioneers of early childhood and focus on how their ideas have been implemented in terms of the resources we select for our baby rooms. By using a wide range of purposeful and meaningfully placed resources to develop the skills conducive to creative thinking, babies will have a varied experience in their settings that will support them in finding their own ideas and being innovative and creative thinkers in the future.

For years, the focus has been on older children in education – namely, those who are eligible for preschool funding – as the government appeared interested only in those who it paid for, ensuring that they were equipped with the best possible education and resources for increasing their 'readiness' for formal schooling and the bigger picture of the eventual place the children will take in society. This is beginning to change in settings, with increased interest in babies and the range of resources and materials they need in order to develop a range of skills and experience a variety of play contexts. Much has been done to advocate for a more child-led approach to learning, and, in turn, this has impacted the types of environments, extra-curricular programmes and resources that we offer to our youngest children in their early years.

The importance of underpinning knowledge

The Baby Room Project, a research project designed and carried out between 2009 and 2012, was helpful in highlighting some of the origins of our understanding and where practitioners get their ideas about resources and the environment from – for example, the well-known idea that babies prefer to look at black-and-white contrasts as this supports their visual development. In fact, as research suggests, it is only in the first few days and weeks of life that this blurred vision occurs and high-contrast images are useful. Most babies start nursery at around the age of six months, by which time their visual capabilities have developed significantly from the initial blurring that is evident in research with newborn infants. As Gooch and Powell (2013:69) state, 'the result (of the black and white concept) has been that many nurseries and particularly baby rooms have areas swathed in black and white fabric with toys to match'.

It is important to note that in no way am I suggesting there is anything wrong with this. We have a treasure basket of black-and-white resources for babies to explore and high-contrast books and imagery in my own setting, but it is also crucial that practitioners understand their why – why is it important to have these resources or not and who do they benefit? Have we created specific spaces with a particular child in mind, or did we simply take a well-known piece of information with little evidence of the benefit to older babies and design a space that looks lovely but serves no purpose? Despite the best intentions of practitioners, without the underpinning knowledge and 'through literal interpretation', it is often the case that spaces and resources are set up in this way. This results in areas of baby rooms that instead of nurturing babies' emerging interests exist solely 'because babies need black and white to see better' or because it looks good.

It is much more helpful to think carefully about the ways in which babies learn and develop according to their interests and evolving physical skills and provide materials and areas within the room that reflect these. Babies need to be fully engaged with interesting items and objects and comfortable in their surroundings in order for them to begin to explore their thinking freely and without hesitation. Veronica Green, an early childhood educator and consultant with significant experience in running her own programme, Ronnie's Pre-School, understands the need to be in tune with young children and provide experiences that develop the whole child through creative use of their senses.

Everyone, especially infants, learn through their senses. Engaging with items such as mirror balls, mason jar lids, and baskets provide opportunities for the whole child to be engaged in a holistic experience. Infants are learning about themselves as individuals, their bodies and

how the world works through multifaceted interactions. Playing with items such as fabrics, containers, napkin rings, cardboard tubes allows for creative exploration with movement, sound, weight, reflection, taste, tactile and visual interactions all at the same time. These materials speak to the infants by provoking ideas and actions. Having the right kinds of materials, space and time to nurture one's creativity starts by laying the foundation in infancy.

RESOURCES FOR BABIES

Think about the range of resources on offer to babies in your setting:

■ How do you define a resource?

■ How do you define what is age appropriate?

■ Do your resources offer challenge and potential to be used in unique ways?

■ Who decides on how the room should be resourced? Are staff consulted?

The resources that are provided for children and the furniture we choose to display them on is a big part of any childcare setting. It takes a lot of time and effort to properly furnish and resource a baby room, and practitioners must always reflect on the reasons why they have made certain choices to ensure that the permanent resources they choose both serve the purposes they are intended for and act as an enhancement to the environment.

Babies should have opportunities to test their physical skills on a regular basis both indoors and out, and there should be a variety of different heights and levels to explore, particularly as they reach the stage of cruising and independent walking. Even if these cannot be featured all of the time, it is important to have beams, boxes and other items that can provide temporary challenge for young children to ensure they have ample opportunities to practice their gross motor skills on a regular basis.

Charlotte Blackburn, the baby room leader at Nina's Nursery High Lane, knows how important it is for children to be offered variety in their experiences and ensures that children in the baby room have the opportunity to explore invitations to learning at different heights.

The resources that we offer our babies play a huge role in the development of creativity; without them, babies may find it difficult to share their creative ideas as they don't yet have a wide range of communicative abilities. There are added pressures when considering resourcing for nonmobile babies and babies who are learning about the world in a very sensory way by using their mouths to explore how various objects taste and feel. With this in mind, it is important to ensure that environments are thoughtfully resourced with a range of interesting items and, of course, supervised closely. Babies who are mouthing objects need to be closely watched, and accessible resources need to be safe for small hands and mouths. Even babies who have moved past the mouthing stage still need a variety of taste-safe options to explore, some of which can be found in part 2 of this book. There are lots of sources of information about the best resources for young babies; books, internet searches and, of course, professional discussions with colleagues will inspire many a practitioner to reach for the catalogues, but many, particularly where budget constraints are an issue, are left feeling like the resources adorning glossy pages of a catalogue are an unachievable dream. Those trying to capitalise on our youngest children, with specific catalogues aimed at the birth-to-two age range, often feature leading quotes from researchers or scientists which makes it difficult for those who are trying to 'withstand market forces' (Goouch & Powell, 2013: 70) to do so while still providing the best care.

Often managers place more importance on resourcing for older age groups, or they get into the habit of buying without consulting practitioners to find out what would be useful or what the children's current interests are. This results in resources that are unused by the children and practitioners who are left feeling devalued as their input is not considered. Instead of reaching for catalogues to buy the latest 'must-have' for your baby room, remember that there are likely lots of items around the setting that can be used to create the same effect. Practitioners need to be mindful that they are a resource too, and by thinking creatively themselves, a world of imagination and invitations to learning can be achieved with the simplest of things.

TOP TIPS FOR RESOURCING YOUR BABY ROOM

- Consider repurposing unwanted furniture around the house (nests of tables, chairs or rugs).

- Remember that children don't have any idea how much something cost – make sure it serves the purpose it was intended for.

- If there is something from a catalogue you think will benefit the children, consider a used toy/book sale or car boot sale – selling on your much-loved resources or items you no longer use could provide valuable budget.

- Ask parents for donations of particular items – they will be more than happy to help if they can.

Resourcing for creativity

So what should be in a baby room? What kinds of resources are best to ignite creative thinking and encourage babies to explore on their own terms? As Duffy (2006:132) states, 'curiosity is a key part of the creative process. If children are not in an environment that excites their curiosity...they will not be creative'. It seems logical then that we must plan effectively the activities, resources, items and objects that will entice children to investigate them, to find out what they do, allowing the children to have their own ideas about how things work and touching on those all-important characteristics of effective learning, ensuring that we provide something for all babies and that will support all learning styles. In their book *The Role of the Adult in Early Years Settings*, Rose and Rogers (2012:121) suggest that 'planning for young children's learning is a highly creative practice' and there is no one size that fits all. We know that free play and child-initiated play chosen by the child is the best way of extending their thinking (Sylva et al., cited in Moyles, 2010). If staff do not plan the environment and resources effectively with high regard for what they know about child development and the children's current interests, the babies will not be motivated to learn, and their exploratory, creative impulses will not be embraced. This has a detrimental impact not only on their learning but more importantly on their emotional well-being and their ability to settle in their environment.

Trying to get the balance right between satisfying leaders with evidence of learning and following a truly child-led, open-ended approach is something that many practitioners find difficult, but it doesn't have to be. By allowing children to fully embrace experiences and by immersing themselves in a particular medium without adult interference, children are able to be joyous in their exploits, something which can often be seen in their body language.

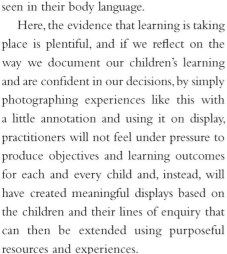

Here, the evidence that learning is taking place is plentiful, and if we reflect on the way we document our children's learning and are confident in our decisions, by simply photographing experiences like this with a little annotation and using it on display, practitioners will not feel under pressure to produce objectives and learning outcomes for each and every child and, instead, will have created meaningful displays based on the children and their lines of enquiry that can then be extended using purposeful resources and experiences.

Authentic resources

Many nurseries around the country are filled with brightly coloured toys that have only one or two ways to play, a preconceived idea that dictates its use and, once mastered, offers very little play value to a young child. If we truly believe that babies are capable, competent human beings, then we have no choice but to believe that these kinds of toys stifle children's creative thinking, which poses the question of why we continue to buy in to these types of resources – in other words, toys that do all the work. There has been an increase in recent years, particularly in the UK, in the return to a more natural, inquisitive baby room, one that features authentic, home-from-home objects of interest instead of shop-bought 'toys', something that Laura from Stone Hen Childcare in Keadby has embraced at her setting:

No doubt a wooden kitchen is a beautiful addition to your role play area but how about thinking out the box and letting our babies use real life objects and media to spur new levels of creativity in their role play. Time for tea? We use a shallow water tray, sliced oranges and cinnamon sticks allowing a multi-sensory experience for babies to flourish their creativity; pouring, scooping, serving and even taste safe for drinking. Ask yourselves how much more creative expression is brought through a real-life experience like this rather than a beautifully painted wooden teapot, sugar cube and cup?

Objects that ignite curiosity in young children and allow open-ended play opportunities are thought to have many benefits to young children when provided alongside other purposeful resources – for example, books, puppets, small-world animals or sensory items. Authentic resources are also favoured because they are extremely accessible in charity shops, car boots in the summer months or even family attics, and they can be unwanted items from family or parents of the setting, which mean they come at a low cost in comparison to the catalogue alternatives.

Providing this range of authentic steel resources in a role play space gives children the opportunity to develop their awareness of texture, temperature of the cold steel and strength as these types of resources are often heavier than plastic. Providing ceramic also instils a sense of confidence in children as they handle it and ensures that from an early age babies are encouraged to handle resources gently as to respect property (something that is a useful life lesson as they grow older) – Squirrels Family and Childcare Centre)

Resources such as these also inspire babies to think creatively as they may be seeing them for the first time and there are no predetermined clues as to their purpose. Of course, risk assessments and common sense have a role to play here in determining what is safe for babies. Heavy teapots and small glass items are not best placed with young babies due to the hazard they pose; however, there is huge value in authentic objects that the plastic alternative cannot provide. Adults have a huge role to play in the way they provide these opportunities to young children, and there is still a huge gap in knowledge amongst practitioners and those coming into the profession about the way we offer and what we offer in terms of resources. Many are not confident enough in their own ability to provide authentic resources for fear of them breaking or little ones getting hurt, but with appropriate, well-thought-out risk assessments and, of course, supervision, babies can learn so much about the world through hands-on experience of real colour, reflective materials, texture and weight of natural and authentic resources.

Treasure baskets

It is important to provide a range of quality resources that also allow the babies in the room to fully explore their schematic patterns of play. Treasure baskets are now seen as part and parcel of a baby room. No doubt there will be at least one in every nursery you have been to or at the very least a collection of objects loosely related. An ever-expanding idea inspired by Elinor Goldschmid, they are a resource that has allowed even the youngest babies to explore freely and in an open-ended way what different groups of objects can do. They provide a rich opportunity to explore properties of items and begin early mathematical categorising amongst the many other benefits. Supporting babies' schematic play is essential for future understanding,

and treasure baskets and their contents are one way that settings are making this a possibility. When babies are engrossed in schema play, they are constantly learning and making connections in their brain which are vital to understanding the world. Treasure baskets also give nonmobile babies autonomy in their play, allowing them to choose what to have and explore on their own terms. Providing lots of opportunity for this type of play enhances their overall development, as they find new ways to interact with objects around them.

We love to enhance an activity like tummy time with a variety of treasure baskets. We love to fill ours with heuristic materials and natural everyday objects so that we can stimulate all five of the senses in play. (Laura Brothwell – Stone Hen Childcare)

For the staff at Nina's Nursery High Lane, mark making also features alongside their collection of authentic resources for young babies to explore during periods of open-ended play:

A practitioner will play alongside the babies and model how to use the objects which is then imitated as shown in the photos of the two babies at the table, one makes marks on their pad with a pencil as if to take notes as the other sits and explores the objects set out for 'tea' and is pictured pretending to sip from a cup and saucer. I feel it is important to offer opportunity for babies to mark make and be creative to their own accord and not just when set out by a practitioner so they feel confident to express themselves in many ways as they grow and become more independent towards their imaginative creativity.

TOP TIPS FOR INTRODUCING AUTHENTIC RESOURCES

■ Introduce one or two items at a time if you are unsure – the children will surprise you with their interest.

■ Some children will need time to learn how to be gentle with authentic materials – take the time to model play and spend time alongside them, commenting on what they are doing and how they have chosen to use an object.

■ Have a look in local charity shops and (in the summer) car boot sales for some bargain finds.

■ China animals make for great realistic small-world play.

■ Wooden curtain or napkin rings on a mug tree keep babies' attention.

■ Try creating a box or basket of resources if you are unsure about having them available all the time – this is helpful while you gain confidence.

The magic properties of dough

Dough is a fantastic resource for young babies because it is extremely versatile, and there are so many variations that can be made with only a few ingredients, most of which early years practitioners have in their cupboards at home. There are a range of scents that can be added as well as herbs, spices and colours to explore, and babies love to squish, squelch, prod and poke dough as it changes shape. Because of this, practitioners at CurioCity Childcare offer dough to their babies regularly.

Adding water or oil and other loose parts also creates another dimension for babies to experiment with sticking things in the dough or feeling the consistency change.

The babies are offered different materials to use during their exploration such as sticks, wooden rings, pinecones and textured pastas to create marks in the playdough alongside their sensory investigation. (Nina's Nursery High Lane)

Dough also provides babies and practitioners the perfect opportunity to explore some of their emerging schemas. Very few other mediums can provide this adaptability, so practitioners have a unique chance to observe many different patterns of play evolve right in front of them. As dough is such a malleable medium, babies can do almost anything to it and the key is to trust the process and watch the magic. During a sensory dough session at Wally's Day Nursery (more information can be found in part 2), babies displayed several schemas throughout and through sensitive support and encouragement from practitioners were able to test their ideas and follow their interests without interference.

Whilst one little boy needed reassurance to get started, the practitioner modelled some of the things they could do with the dough, talking to him calmly until he was ready to venture independently. Some babies explored the marks they could make with their fingers, whilst others were more interested in 'posting' loose parts through an empty spice rack. The little boy who initially needed encouragement, having gained confidence in his own ability and the knowledge that the adults around him trust his process, decided to fully immerse himself in the experience by climbing up onto the table. Notice here an example of the 'why not?' philosophy. He wasn't hurting anyone, and with close supervision he wasn't going to get hurt, so why not let him explore, test his physical skills and gain confidence in what he is trusted to do.

Babies at Stone Hen Childcare also use their dough in inventive ways with stamping and poking tools to change the shape of their dough alongside freshly cut fruits to add to the sensory experience. These kinds of tools can also be used with other mediums to great sensory effect.

Art-based materials

> The freedom, curiosity, and sense of adventure with which young children approach art
> is very difficult to relearn once it has been squelched. (Striker, 2001: 3)

The use of art-based materials is something that has become commonplace in nurseries and childminding settings but is still handled with hesitation by some, particularly with babies. Offering babies a range of thought-provoking, stimulating materials from an early age ensures that they experience the world in a holistic way. Only when they are provided with such materials and uninterrupted time can babies begin to express themselves freely, explore their senses and engage in critical thinking.

> Just as infants need nutrition for the development of their physical and mental health, they
> too need creativity to nourish their cognitive development and well-being. Stimulating
> all of the senses in infancy is key to their learning and understanding of the world around
> them. When we give infants the right materials, and time to explore we can expand on

their natural proclivity towards creative thinking. Infants and toddlers should be given materials of varying textures, scents, colors, and sound making abilities, in order to help them reach their full developmental potential. (Ashley Corcoran, Love of Learning Childcare)

It is so important that practitioners working with young babies and children understand the impact that their own views can have on the children they work with and that they echo the ethos of the setting they are a part of. If there is a tension between what an individual believes to be the right way to do something and the values of the setting, they cannot work together to provide a consistent experience and will potentially be at odds with other members of staff. These thoughts will have an impact also on the types of art materials, paints, glue and the huge range of other media available that are provided and how they are used and subsequently 'allowed' to be used by babies.

As mindful practitioners, we need to be wary of the materials we offer to babies and ensure they have been assessed for risk before being offered. This has become part of our role, particularly when working with such young children; however, this has stopped many from offering materials such as glue or shaving foam because of the risk or the perception of others.

As an adult, we know that we shouldn't taste glue, shaving foam, nonedible paint and dough, but babies do not yet have this thinking and are interested only in finding out. Often baby room practitioners will cloud a creative activity with 'no, don't eat that' or 'don't put that in your mouth' or worse, not provide the opportunity at all. 'Creative thinking involves a fresh approach and original ideas' (Striker, 2001: 7), and children as young as six months have already formed patterns of behaviour that can be difficult to undo. It is so important that attitudes towards exploratory learning are open to all that this encompasses – including the mess and occasional coloured nappy. A child would need to ingest a large amount of glue or paint to make it dangerous, and there are now nontoxic varieties available, giving very little excuse to avoid such an endeavour. If a practitioner is close by supervising (which I strongly recommend), then there is a minimal possibility that a young child will manage to ingest the entire pot, and the subsequent learning that takes place far outweighs the risk involved.

The same argument can be used for almost all art-based materials: crayons, shaving foam, paint, clay, dough; many would argue they have no place in a baby room since most babies mouth objects, paint and glue is too dangerous and they would just eat the crayons or shredded paper. To some extent this may be true; however, I would argue that if done thoughtfully, there is a huge amount of enjoyment that comes from allowing and even encouraging this type of exploration. Confident practitioners who are able to assess the risk and offer these opportunities anyway often know the benefits of early mark making,

using senses to explore and investigating texture and the importance of exposing children to a range of materials.

Messy creative play is a great opportunity for babies to explore using all five of their senses. Foam and sand are perfect for investigating how we can create marks and prints, and we love to let our babies explore bare foot not only in the sand, on the grass or in mud but also when experiencing creative play. There are no right or wrong materials to use but pasta in every form is always a go to in our provision. Printing with left over fruits and vegetables is a great differentiation to brushes and stampers when supporting babies in creative play especially, practicing those vital pre-writing palmer and pincer grasps. (Laura Brothwell – Stone Hen Childcare)

Bright Stars Nursery in Sunderland also introduce their young babies to creative experiences daily, offering a range of materials to use independently or with support:

> Not only do we use a range of natural, open ended and challenging resources but we encourage our children to explore these materials on a variety of surfaces.

By encouraging children to access art materials and resources and use them in innovative ways on a variety of surfaces, practitioners can support young children's understanding of colour, texture, marks and strokes as well as develop their fine and gross motor skills.

In part 2, we will look at various recipes and methods of making paints, doughs and other baby-safe art materials, and there are some great ideas online, on platforms such as Pinterest and other social media sites too. Often they are cheap to make, and many have ingredients that we all have at the back of the cupboard at home.

TOP TIPS FOR MAKING ART

- Start small if you need time to adjust to the process of art making – chalks, chunky crayons and even paintbrushes with water on black paper are a great way to begin mark making with young children.

- Be prepared – have buckets ready for washing babies after the activity (particularly body painting) and nappies/clothes nearby.

- Ensure you have enough of each resource and regularly stock paints or powder paints and glue.

■ If making a baby-safe medium, make sure this is prepared and ready to use when babies need it.

■ Have a range of mediums available (shaving foam, paint, clay, dough, etc.), and think about how these can be presented to children so that they are curious to explore.

■ For children who may be hesitant – try adding their favourite objects or small-world toys – this will spark their interest and encourage them to have a go.

Food as a resource

As Susan Striker (2001:58) suggests, '"Don't play with your food" does not make any sense to a child of this age'. Babies who are sitting up are interested in everything: reaching out, touching and finding out about the world in the most sensory way they know. Allowing children the freedom to explore food supports them in learning 'about the nature and physical properties of food and develop motor coordination, which will develop into drawing and writing and creates a healthy attitude about being allowed to satisfy curiosity' (Striker, 2001: 58).

I am not advocating for letting young babies play with their food instead of eating it, and it is usually best to leave this type of experimenting for when a baby is not hungry (as this may cause unnecessary distress); however, food will inevitably become only for eating when babies are introduced to other mark-making materials at the appropriate time, so it really should not be something staff worry about. 'Children take great joy when they mess –and are learning – and it should not make adults uncomfortable' (Striker, 2001: 60); sadly, it does for many who often don't like mess themselves. This thinking that mealtimes or food are only for eating is impacting the way young children explore and experience the world, and without this vital experience, our babies are lacking the opportunity to freely explore the world the way nature intended them to.

Accessible resources

There are a few key features that are apparent within most creative environments for babies, including good-quality, open-ended resources, plenty of time to explore freely, well-placed colour and novelty objects and, one that causes some controversy, the apparent need for accessible resources. This is, in my opinion, personal preference and will often fit with the ethos and values of a setting.

There is no right or wrong way to store materials as long as babies have access to them and adults around them can respond sensitively to their interests and needs. For example, in my own setting, creative resources such as brushes, sponges, mark-making implements and tools are stored in lidded, transparent boxes where babies can see them. Older babies can access these independently, and younger babies are able to show their interest in the contents, often observed by practitioners who then safely provide the experience alongside paint, dough or other malleable materials.

It is important to remember that spaces that are for children should be just that, for children. This means that they should be as clutter-free as possible. When we talk about accessible resources, that doesn't mean everything in the room. When organising resources, adult belongings should always be stored away from babies and young children. Their naturally inquisitive, creative minds could do a lot with the contents of a handbag! Paperwork and files that are of no use to the children and other adult-only items should be out of reach and preferably out of sight, but this will depend on your individual workspace and the storage solutions that you have in place.

Getting down to a child's level and looking at the environment from their perspective can be revealing in terms of the overall feeling of a space and is helpful before making decisions based on your own perspective rather than that of the child. We know from research that babies thrive in calm, natural environments with the opportunity to explore resources that are accessible to them. Overly busy, cluttered or artificial environments are known to affect behaviour in young children and have a detrimental impact on their development, so these are worth reflecting on regularly as it is easy to become complacent. Low wooden or transparent boxes and neutral tones seek to create a sense of calm within baby rooms and ensure that resources are accessible. Having resources low enables younger babies to access their own resources independently and older babies to make selections based on what they can see.

TOP TIPS FOR MAKING RESOURCES ACCESSIBLE

- Discuss as a team what level of accessibility you can manage, and take steps to make this happen – this applies to all resources.

- Wooden boxes or crates are a great way to provide items such as treasure baskets so that even young babies can access them freely.

- Consider a basket of puppets or props near to a cosy space for babies to explore.

- Art materials can be stored on a trolley that can be brought out or can be placed on low shelves for babies to share their interest.

- Malleable materials such as dough can be set up as an invitation to explore alongside a tea set or bowls and spoons.

- Mirrors and reflective materials should be arranged close to the ground so that young babies on their back or front can see themselves and explore the reflective properties.

- Keeping shelves free of adult paperwork and files leaves more space to set up miniature provocations for those babies who can pull to stand or walk around furniture.

Conclusions

You shouldn't feel deflated or feel you have to make huge sudden changes to your environments, you as the teacher are partners in your babies creative learning, without that invaluable bond and interaction between adult and child, no provocation or wonder rich environment/activity will have the creative learning outcomes you set to achieve. (Laura Brothwell, Stone Hen Childcare)

Young children should be free to explore the world through their senses. There are so many ways to experience and engage with art, and encouraging creative thinking is easy when you understand your why. Simply offering resources is not enough, although it is a great start. As the adult role model, it is important that we understand the benefit of free exploration and set aside any preconceived ideas and thoughts of an end product. Babies are not so much interested in what they do, just how they do it, and more importantly that they were allowed to do it. Babies should be free to smear paint, manipulate materials, independently access the things that motivate them and conduct their own research into the materials that are available.

7 Exploring outdoors

Introduction

In this final chapter of part 1, we will look at the importance of the outdoors and some of the influences that have shaped the way we offer outdoor play to young children. We will also delve into the crucial role that parents play in their child's experience of nature and the perception children develop as a result as well as the importance of practitioners in sharing with children the wonders of being outdoors and providing a wealth of experiences that are appropriate for babies. As Laura from Stone Hen Childcare suggests, 'being outside gives babies a whole new experience to our natural world. A chance to see and witness, first-hand the magic of the world around them, providing a pure sense of freedom to explore and investigate'.

It is our responsibility to ensure that the babies we care for have the opportunity to experience the natural world and its many benefits every day, and this chapter will provide some insight into how to set up the environment, what to provide and how to get the best from your space.

Why being outdoors is so important

There is a huge amount of evidence to suggest that being outdoors is the most natural way in which children learn. At a time when screens and sedentary lifestyles seem to be taking over, adults and children alike are often caught up in a whirlwind of social engagements and busy schedules. Sadly, our babies and young children are suffering and so too is their creativity. With more and more parents increasingly tech savvy, filling their homes with the latest technology, coupled with the rise in house prices, rent and living costs, many children are growing up in flats without gardens and in urban environments. Local parks and woodlands are available, but these go undiscovered as many families don't have the time or transport to get to them. It falls to early years practitioners, settings and childminders then to ensure that children know the wonder these places can provide and that young children have regular opportunities to explore nature.

According to their article, Slade, Lowery and Bland (2013: 66) suggest that there is concern nationally about children's 'engagement in outdoor play' and the growing risk of 'nature deficit disorder'. This could be for a number of reasons. Increased urbanization of the countryside means that fewer children have access to grassed areas, and a bigger transport network means that walking as a mode of transport has been replaced by a bus, car or train journey, so active engagement with the outdoors is limited. For babies confined to car seats or pushchairs, parents now spend their journeys with headphones in or on their phones, no longer engaging with their babies, commenting on the natural wonders that they see as they walk. This is echoed by McKinney (2012: 24) as she states, 'the ability to explore in nature alone is not a common activity for children today', and she goes on to cite research that suggests 'our capitalist, corporate and industrialised societies have limited the roaming abilities of children'. That is why nurseries have such an important part to play in enriching the lives of young children, as it may be the only opportunity that they get to be outdoors.

Outdoor learning, forest school and Nordic influences

This idea of the child as an 'active agent' is rapidly becoming a new way of thinking about children, and the different constructions of childhood that have been evidenced throughout this book suggest that this shift is a positive one, where the child has much more control over their learning. The way we think about learning and the context in which it takes place needs to change, particularly with regard to young children, if this shift in thinking is to have an impact. The introduction of the forest school concept means there has been an increase in the number of children accessing a wider range of experiences so that 'children engage in activities within their social world' (Fleer, 2010: 21). As Dahlberg et al. (2007: 66) point out, 'since our construction of the child determines the institutions we provide for children', there needs to be a new way of thinking about the places and environments that are used in the education of our youngest children and their significance in terms of the benefit they provide.

This is where the Nordic countries have acted as inspiration for the West. The concept of 'Friluftsliv (fresh air life)' (Knight cited in Maynard & Waters, 2014: 87) is something which is embedded within the Nordic culture. 'Being outside in wilder places is a normal part of many young children's lives', and they grow up surrounded by it. Just pause for a moment and think about the concept of 'fresh air life'. Is that not something we should all want for our children? Free from the constraints of a screen and the anxieties about being outdoors in all weathers – free to just be, to reflect on the world and get back to our roots in the natural environment. However, this is still a somewhat alien concept to many practitioners within the UK, predominantly as 'video games and television keep children indoors and thus contribute to a reduction of children's independent outdoor experiences' (Lindemann-Matthies & Knecht, 2011: 152). In her own book, Knight (2013: 6) states that

> the cultural norm is of regular access to the environment for the majority of the population, so attitudes to the practicalities of risk-taking, campfires, knives and so on are very different from those of the majority of the population of the UK.

McKinney (2012: 26) talks of other activities, particularly in relation to being outdoors, that are 'seen as unfathomable for school boards' as they would be 'constantly imagining lawsuits and liability issues'. This may not seem relevant to the babies in our settings; however, the idea that practitioners are worried about the risks involved with taking infants out into the woodland is one that should not be ignored. There is a red-tape culture in this country that seems nonexistent in others, making it difficult to really experience outdoor learning, particularly with such young children, and what it stands for in its entirety. There could be many reasons for this, including concerns over staff-child ratio, transport, staff confidence and unpredictability of behaviour. Again, many of these are based on a particular setting's policies and procedures. Thankfully, managers and leaders are beginning to take back the reins in terms of what services they are choosing to offer families and in using their professional judgement can risk assess any potential outdoor adventure. That said, there are very few settings apart from those who identify as true forest school or outdoor provision that take their youngest children out regularly. There is evidence of this in my own setting: when potential parents visit for a tour of our setting and we discuss outdoor learning, they are almost stunned that our under threes go out two or three times weekly, sometimes more.

As the Play Safety Forum (2002) state, 'all children (whatever their age) both need and want to take risks in order to explore limits, venture into new experiences and develop their capacities' (cited in Else, 2012: 25), and as this idea becomes more accepted through extensive research, so too is the idea of risk taking as part of being outdoors in the natural world (under supervision from qualified, sensitive adults). This is so important for children under two as they are at the perfect age, exploring their capabilities and finding out about what their bodies can do. Being in nature provides some amazing opportunities that many young children are missing out on because practitioners are unable or unwilling to take them out.

Parental engagement

An 'important factor that limits children's autonomy outdoors is parental anxiety' (Huttenmoser et al., Valentine & Kendrick cited in Lindemann-Matthies & Knecht, 2011: 152). This is certainly the case with such young children, as they are very susceptible to behaviour changes and quickly learn what is expected of them. Parents and the anxieties they have play a large part in determining the way in which their children respond to the outdoors, and being unable to act autonomously is not conducive to a child-centered approach as it can never be about the child. Parents can inadvertently project their fears onto their children, who in return learn to fear the unknown, ultimately limiting their experience in the outdoors. 'Parents…pass on their culture and beliefs, either consciously or accidentally' (Else, 2012: 19), and in all walks of life this is inevitable; however, problems can arise and have a lasting impact on the child when parents do not take into account the best interests of their child.

This can be described in terms of parenting styles. Else (2012: 20) claims that one effect of 'hyper-parenting' is that 'children will have little time to be truly themselves'. We have already discovered how detrimental this can be to a child's ability to be creative. He adds, 'the results of this approach… precocious children who don't know how to make friends and play with their peers'. This is evident in settings where children can play in a solitary manner and often go unnoticed. These are the children who are unable to share ideas effectively or use their imaginations in a group (something vital for creativity). In the context of an outdoor environment, however, it is not as easily hidden. Children who have been parented in this way are often the children who become 'lost' in the forest; they are unable to pick up on play cues from other children and struggle to adapt their play to the environment.

Similarly, it is also evident which children have had a more relaxed upbringing. In their case, however, they will be used to and even 'overly confident with' (Else, 2012: 20) familiar resources but 'resistant to experience new activities or new situations'. Else goes on to suggest that a 'balance' is needed in order to get the best from a given situation, where 'children will tend to have a broad range of play experiences and will tend to be confident across the range' (Else, 2012: 20).

TOP TIPS FOR INCLUDING PARENTS

■ Offer words of encouragement to parents who may be unsure about what to expect from your outdoor provision.

■ Show them photographs of the babies in a range of places, exploring a range of resources.

■ Support them in understanding that the outdoors is important for all areas of learning and shouldn't be viewed as an extension of the indoors.

■ Invite parents for a stay-and-play session in your outdoor environment; this way they can see first-hand what happens outdoors.

■ Share observations or photographs of their child outside – they are more likely to get onboard with the idea of outdoor play in all weathers if they see evidence of their child enjoying it.

■ Be mindful of those families who may not have the means to provide warm clothing, boots or spare clothes. Ensure you have at least two spare sets so that no baby misses the opportunity to be outside.

Only when parents understand the benefit of such a rich, resourceful environment can you begin to work together to ensure children regain their natural instinct to play, be curious and return to nature.

Go outside! Children (even babies) burn a lot of energy, they need space to move, climb and practice their physical skills. Expecting babies and young children to play indoors for hours each day is difficult for them and you! Take the indoors outside and watch many of your behaviour issues disappear. Younger and younger children now spend their lives cooped up inside, in cars, at scheduled activities, on iPads and watching screens. Nature Deficit Disorder is a very real thing amongst the children of today, open your doors and let the children play! (Carlene Cox-Newton)

The role of the practitioner outdoors

As with many aspects of baby care and supporting the development of creativity within it, the practitioner's role in facilitating and respecting the child's interests is crucial. This is even more relevant outdoors and is somewhat easier to achieve, since their interests are usually based on what they are experiencing at any given moment. In order to become developmentally supportive of the child and their captivations while outdoors, practitioners must have 'respect for the child's choices underpinned by an understanding of and commitment to children's wisdom in relation to their learning needs' (Malaguzzi (1993) cited in O'Connor 2012:6), and this respect is a pedagogical principle that is found in the pioneering philosophies of Montessori, Steiner and Malaguzzi amongst others.

Most settings now have outdoor spaces, although this is not a requirement of the early years foundation stage framework. How these are organised can differ greatly between settings and is usually dependent on the size of the provision (and the outdoor space), the number of children and staff to supervise them as well as making sure, particularly in day nurseries, that all of the children have the opportunity to play outside every day. Factor in the ongoing pressure on practitioners to evidence their learning on display boards and in planning folders, and it is easy to see why the outdoors often doesn't get the focus it deserves.

In creating spaces outdoors, some settings choose to partition their youngest children using fences or gateways to give them a safe space to play and explore without worrying about the boisterous activities of older children. Others operate shared access, and many are now combining their children regardless of age to ensure that young children have the opportunity to mix and form beneficial relationships with their peers and children in other rooms. Practitioners need to ensure they provide access to a wide range of good-quality resources and that they are planning mindfully, creating a balance between child-initiated opportunities and invitations to investigate. (Reflections Nursery and Small School)

For those who don't have an outdoor area of their own or one that is limited, visiting local parks, garden centres and other local areas of interest becomes a daily occurrence in a bid to ensure children are experiencing as much of the natural world as possible. For babies, this often means being transported in slings or prams, watching the world go by as they are wheeled or carried through it, but why is this? Is it because they can't walk, or is it simply a means of getting the children from A to B? The answers to these questions are entirely dependent on the practitioners and the culture they have created in their settings alongside the importance they have placed on being outdoors. If practitioners don't appreciate the benefits that the outdoors has to offer, participation will be minimal, affecting the children they have with them so much so that babies may not even get out of their

prams. We have got to start thinking differently if we are to ensure that all babies experience the world and everything it has to offer. Practitioners are in the best position to introduce babies to the wonders of nature, and we are beginning to see change. We are increasingly seeing that for many types of provision, there is a focus on returning to nature, both indoors with the use of natural loose parts and the idea of using more recycled materials and outdoors, as we learn about the impact being in nature has on well-being and young children's overall development.

At Squirrels Family and Childcare Centre, staff make every effort to take the children out daily and ensure that the learning they experience along the way is valuable and meaningful to the children:

As part of our daily practice we visit local woodlands, farms, parks and anywhere within reasonable distance for our location. From day one we build up the children's stamina for walking and resilience for being able to walk and cope with longer distances. Throughout the nursery, from when children are stable on their feet we encourage them to walk alongside the buggy and enjoy the freedom of being able to walk independently. We also make these visits to local places to build up the children's ability to cope with changes in the environment, questioning and experiencing a variety of terrain and atmosphere. This, in turn, means the children have to learn the health and safety aspects around them; be aware

of any dangers for example crossing roads, touching animals and washing hands afterwards. In visiting local places regularly, we also build a sense of community, people recognise the staff and children and often engage in conversation, greeting and adding to their experience further. We are very well known to many local businesses and places in our village and town.

This example gives hope to those who do not have a dedicated outdoor area and shows that when practitioners and leaders place value on outdoor experiences, the children reap the benefits of regular access to their environment.

Day nurseries that operate from houses, on the other hand, may have outdoor provision available, but they often place babies upstairs. According to Clare (2012), many nurseries do this because older children can then enjoy free flow play to the outdoors, but why is it any more important for them than for the babies? Is it because it is easier to open

the door and simply let them go? She argues, 'Where are the rights of the very young children to this access?' (Clare, 2012:75). Even when mixed age ranges have access to the same outdoor space, there is the question of resources appropriate for different age groups and the safety of the babies when there are older, more robust children running around freely. Like many things, this comes down to the practitioners. It doesn't matter what space you have available, it is what you do with it that matters the most to those who use it. It is the practitioner's role to ensure that the babies are safe, stimulated and able to enjoy everything the outdoors has to offer throughout the year (and not just when the sun is out).

TOP TIPS FOR HARD-TO-REACH SPACES

- ▪ If you do not have free flow access:

  - Ensure high priority is given to having uninterrupted time outside planned into the morning and afternoon.

  - Plan in the morning what resources need to be outside and take them out before the children arrive (this will save multiple trips).

  - Schedule outdoor play days where the children have access to the outdoors for whole sessions.

- ▪ If you have a small outdoor space:

  - Utilise walls and fences for hooks and hanging baskets. Mark-making materials such as chalkboards, clipboards and weaving panels don't take up any space when flat to a wall.

  - Try to keep planters and seating to the outside, leaving space to play in the middle.

  - If you have a very small space, think reflectively about the seasons and utilise themes rather than trying to offer too much that is not of a high quality.

  - Ensure there are plants and greenery to give the feeling of nature all around the children.

  - Think carefully about what you want to offer the children, ensuring there is difference from being indoors.

- ▪ If you do not have provision for outdoors:

  - Risk assess local walks, fields or nearby play areas.

  - Ask for parent volunteers who are almost always happy to help where they can.

  - Take the children puddle splashing or on listening walks with cameras to capture their experience.

  - Make sure that the outdoors is always high on the agenda.

Benefits of outdoor play

Many of the pioneers we have already discovered have in some way advocated for the benefits of being outdoors and learning in the most natural environment of them all. We know that children need to play and have uninterrupted time to experience their world, developing their spatial awareness, skills in movement and sensory stimulation.

There is also very little focus on what the children have to achieve and what outcomes are being met whilst they are outdoors; instead, focus on providing a true sense of exploration on the child's terms and with their immediate interests and fascinations in mind. Rinaldi suggests that 'the potential of a child is stunted when the endpoint of their learning is formulated in advance' (1993: 104), and this is something that is almost never the case when engaging in the moment outdoors. Children have the opportunity, when the appropriate support is in place, to take different aspects of the outdoors and use them creatively.

Sensory benefits

When children are given unstructured time outdoors, they have the opportunity to experience at their own pace the rich sensory input that nature provides. It not only encourages curiosity, exploration, understanding and self-regulation but also provides the ideal learning environment for even the smallest infants, as all of their senses are engaged. Research shows that babies need a sensory-rich environment that features a variety of textures, temperatures, colours, smells and sounds.

One of my all-time favourite things to do outdoors with children of any age is to take their shoes and socks off and share with them the joy of crawling or walking through wet grass.

There are so many sensory benefits to being barefoot outdoors, but for lots of children, they have never experienced this joy. This is mainly due to the sedentary lifestyle that their parents have created, so even going outside, let alone with no shoes on, is not something that is often considered. Being barefoot develops a child's sensory, motor and executive functions and stimulates receptors in the feet that would otherwise not be touched.

Unsurprisingly, due to the lack of free time spent in the wild, particularly at a young age when babies are often confined to their pushchairs or wrapped in cotton wool for fear of being hurt, this lack of movement can have catastrophic effects in later years and has been shown to 'leave children underprepared for academics and overwhelmed by daily life and social situations' (Hanscom, 2016: 3). It is more important than ever to get babies outside; nature is the ultimate sensory experience, and failure to connect with it from a young age leads to an array of problems, as we have seen.

Impact of restricted access to outdoors

In her book *Balanced and Barefoot*, Angela Hanscom (2016) describes some of the problems that today's children are facing because of restricted access to the outdoors. She discusses children's decreasing core strength, poor posture due to increased sitting in restrictive chairs and devices, decreased stamina and trouble with spatial awareness, all of which can be avoided with regular time outside.

It is a common misconception that children get ill from being outdoors, but this is something that stops many parents and practitioners from allowing their children out, particularly in the winter months if they have been unwell for some time. Parents need to be educated not only on the benefits for their child's physical development but also for their health. Lack of time spent outdoors is actually to blame for increased illness in young children: 'children also develop weakened immune systems and are prone to colds, illnesses and allergies' (Hanscom, 2016:22).

Encourage parents to dress the children warmly, and they can continue to enjoy being outside in all weathers; this goes for adults too. Get a hat, scarf, gloves and warm coat, and find joy in going outside with babies. We have all seen and known those practitioners who love to play outside in the sunshine but then refuse to take the children out when it gets cold. If you are prepared for the weather and dress yourself as you expect the children to be, you are ensuring that the children still benefit from being outside and are acting as a role model (especially for babies who like to take hats and gloves off repeatedly). As practitioners, we do have a duty of care to our youngest children, and for this reason it is important to ensure that you take at least one blanket, spare clothes in case the children get wet and an extra hat, scarf and gloves to warm cold hands and add extra layers, especially to those who are nonmobile as they will have difficulty in maintaining their temperature and find it difficult to warm up with the lack of movement.

REFLECTION

- Discuss in a group your policies and procedures for outdoor play. Who decides what happens during the time spent outdoors? Is it free flow access or a set session? Why?

- Now think about your community spaces. When was the last time the children went into the local community? Was it planned or spontaneous and were there any restrictions?

- When discussing your provision for outdoors, it is important that you reflect on current practice and evaluate whether there is anything more that can be done.

CASE STUDY - OUTDOOR LEARNING AT WALLY'S DAY NURSERY

Based on a large industrial estate in the centre of a town, the outdoor area at my setting is not the biggest. We are a large day nursery catering for up to seventy children on a daily basis, and we have worked hard to utilise every bit of space that we have to maximum effect.

Our space is comprised of a decked area covered in artificial grass on one level (that our babies have free flow access to throughout the morning), a concrete area on a lower level with mud kitchen and an alleyway that connects our three buildings. It can be difficult to ensure that the babies have a range of natural experiences. We have utilised a portion of the alleyway and transformed it into a sensory path (details in part 2) to be used by all the children, and we always ensure that there are a range of resources available for the babies to explore and investigate on the upper level, often bringing resources from inside to the outside or using what is available in our choosing shed (a large structure with shelves of resources for our various age groups).

Sometimes, though, this is not enough, largely because despite our well-placed planters, grass doesn't grow on concrete, and it is for that reason that we take every opportunity that we can to go out into the community to experience the natural world. Recognising and acting on limitations is a huge part of reflective practice, something that we pride ourselves on. We know and understand our limitations being a setting on an industrial estate and do everything we can to ensure the babies in our care get the best natural outdoor experiences available.

In our baby room, we collect and source natural baby-safe loose parts such as sticks, acorns, pinecones, conkers (under supervision) and tree bark as well as a range of leaves in different shapes, sizes and colours. In the springtime we fill the room with flowers for the children to enjoy, both to look at and touch as well as to use in their play (whether mixed with shaving foam, for potions with coloured water or in corn flour). We have a large array of wooden bricks

and stacking shapes as well as wooden rings on a mug tree and wooden animals, bringing the different colours and shades of nature indoors (often paired with stories to support learning).

We are extremely lucky to have a local garden centre with large grassed area and fenced pond as well as three local parks with a range of play equipment and fields. The children visit these regularly on a ratio that we feel adequately supervises the children whilst allowing them to explore the environment freely. Whether the babies walked, rode in a pram or were carried via sling, once they reach their destination they are always taken out and placed on

the ground. From the first minute they touch the ground, they are free to explore any way they choose. If the weather allows, we encourage the children to spend some of the time barefoot to enjoy the benefits described above. Babies need the opportunity to feel different textures and terrains, which will help and support them to become more stable on their feet. Once they can stand confidently, they will often pull to stand on trees, feeling the bark and trunks of the trees.

Babies will visit the library and enjoy river walks and puddle splashing on the wetter days and when back at nursery, practitioners work hard to provide stimulating play spaces, creating dens and cosy corners as well as obstacle courses for the older babies.

Moreover, we purchased a minibus to take our children (including our babies, of course) to the local woodland, where they can experience a whole range of sensory encounters including barefoot walks and sleeping in the outdoors. We celebrate Outdoor Classroom Day twice a year, taking the whole nursery outdoors for the day. We are lucky to have secured a weekly spot at the local woodland, and on these days we can spend up to eight hours outside, enjoying a lunch cooked on the firepit and rest time in woodland dens.

CASE STUDY – STONE HEN CHILDCARE

In this case study, Laura describes how she views the environment and subsequently uses it as a resource with the babies at her setting to ensure they have a range of thought-provoking sensory experiences. She also shares insight into a new accreditation based on the principle of Hygge, a Danish word that, although not translated into English, represents the concept of being calm and reflective and finding awe and wonder in the little things in life (something which babies are extremely good at).

Giving babies access to the outdoor environment is priceless. Experiencing first-hand, the delights of nature will inspire babies and can do nothing but only flourish creative thinking and expression.

Through my training and continued professional development, I stumbled across the wonderful Hygge in the Early Years Accreditation and a beautiful quote from Kimberly Smith that has without a doubt changed my practice and thought process when working with babies and young children. Forest bathing simply means immersing yourself in a forest setting. It is a natural way to calm your senses in a busy world. It originated in Japan in the 1980s, where it is translated as 'shrining you'. Research has shown that forest bathing and connecting with nature measurably reduces stress levels. This is not only good for your mental health but it leads to many improvements in many aspects of your physical health, including a boost to your immune system. It also frees up your creativity and problem-solving capabilities along with improving your mood. You will often find me and the babies stumbling across the woodland tracks, feeding our creativity's instinct by finding the most beautiful back drops to create marks in the mud, design instruments with our sticks, painting with stream water and just taking in our beautiful surroundings.

Back in our provision garden we love to use homegrown produce – herbs, vegetables and fruits – to inspire creativity and empower our babies through their play! Embedding a culture of sustainability throughout our practice. We are dedicated to spreading this message to our children's parents, carers and member of our community so everyone can continue these opportunities at home with fantastic results. We are regularly gifted seeds by local farmers to share with our families and often trade and swap our home grown produce and creative ideas giving parents and babies the chance to be fully involved in the learning process in and out of provision.

Through these two case studies, we can see very different outdoor environments utilised to provide the best-quality experiences for the children. The most important aspect here is not the spaces we have but what we do with them to ensure that there are a range of experiences, colours, sensory input and stimulating opportunities for babies to explore freely.

Creating an outdoor space for babies

Whilst not every setting has access to a fantastic or large outdoor space, and regardless of whether it is segregated from older children, what is important is that practitioners regularly reflect on the area available, ensure it is equipped to provide the best possible outdoor experience to children and utilise the space they have to maximum effect.

Resources for the outdoors are relatively easy to come by, and there are lots of recyclable materials that can be put to use in all weathers. Crates, boxes, pallets, decking planks and tyres are all great for the outdoors – they can be used for obstacle courses for babies who are on their feet and ready to explore their gross motor movements confidently or as features of the environment (tyres for planters or sand pits, decking planks for low-level seating). Having different-sized fabrics available and pegs or string also means that staff can create dens easily if they are not readily available in the space.

Practitioners can also provide a range of mobile resources ready to be taken outdoors. This could include treasure baskets with noise makers and tools for banging on different surfaces; mark making materials such as chalks, large crayons or paintbrushes (great for making marks on walls with a bucket of water); or even a collection of board books to enjoy inside a cosy nook. For nonmobile babies or those cruising but not walking, resources that focus on reflections are fantastic for use outdoors. Mirrors will reflect the sky or surrounding greenery for children to enjoy. Exploring textures using sensory trays is perfect for little fingers and toes.

If you have the space, providing somewhere for older babies where they can invent and experiment with ideas is a great way to instil self-confidence and trust as well as inspiring and sharing with them a sense of awe and wonderment in the environment. This is something that the staff at Bright Stars Nursery have done particularly well by creating an outdoor art studio.

Our outdoor art studio is heavily influenced by nature and our changing seasons. Staff use what is available within our beyond for our children to explore and create with and children regularly go foraging. Our mud kitchen is fully equipped with utensils to challenge our children's thought processes, along with a range of seasonal materials found in nature to experiment with.

Looking for innovative ways to improve spaces and make the most of areas that are underused, such as hanging baskets filled with resources for mark making, adding guttering to unsightly walls as a water wall or simply adding pots and pans for the children to initiate their own band can all add to the opportunities that babies have while outdoors.

TOP TIPS FOR MAKING THE MOST OF YOUR OUTDOOR SPACE

■ Make it someone's responsibility to check the outdoor area each day and get out stored resources – this way they are ready for the children to play with.

■ Nonmobile babies will need to be taken outside daily. (Make sure they are wrapped up warm in the winter and kept shaded in the summer.)

■ If you have concrete or hard surfaces outdoors, consider covering at least some of the area with a rug to provide comfort for younger babies and a soft surface for them to lie on their backs and watch the sky.

■ Consider the use of mirrors outdoors as this will make the space feel bigger and provide another perspective for young babies.

■ Offer resources and materials at different heights for babies to practice their growing physical skills.

And finally, if you have the opportunity to use a local space or grass area, you should take it at every opportunity – there are not enough children crawling and running free in nature, and if we have any hope of changing this, we need to show them how much fun it can be if we all just put a little more effort in.

Part 2

8 Let the babies play: Invitations

Introduction

In this second part of the book, I will provide some great ideas and invitations to develop creativity for the youngest children in our childcare settings. I have worked with babies throughout my career, and along the way I have learned a lot about how they engage with what adults provide for them and what they choose for themselves. I have studied the way in which they explore and investigate the world around them in their own unique way, and in this part of the book I will share some insight into what I have learnt, based on sound knowledge of how babies develop in their earliest months through to their second birthday and the practical experiences they encounter in early years settings.

Babies are innately very curious, inquisitive human beings. Throughout part 1, we have looked at different aspects of the environment that help to support and develop creativity and have explored the resources and more importantly the relationships that are needed to provide every baby with the foundations for developing their early creative skills.

When young children are absorbed in what they are doing, they will have high levels of involvement and are able to select their resources independently and use them in a range of ways. Babies will begin to understand simple concepts through unhurried time exploring experiences and will develop their self-esteem, confidence and problem-solving skills. It is important to think very carefully about what we believe to be true about babies, the way we should engage with them and what we believe them to be capable of in order for us to provide the best possible experiences. Throughout the course of this book, I hope I have provided some thought-provoking questions in relation to your own practice with the babies in your care.

Before we delve into a range of invitations to play and create, it is important to first define what we mean by these types of activities. In the early years, it is very easy, particularly in a baby room, to fall into the practical routines that are set by management and/or room leaders. We know babies need to be well nourished and have adequate sleep in order for them to be in the best emotional state for play. We also know it is vital that babies have a range of stimulating experiences throughout their day (with time to reflect and be solitary if they choose) married with routines that are essential for growth and development, such as meal and sleep times. We often refer to these experiences as activities, but what do we really mean? An activity is anything that a baby spends time doing, whether this is self-chosen or facilitated by adults. It accounts for almost anything where a baby's brain is active, either through practicing physical skills or looking at books. Invitations to play are just that, resources or items that have been chosen and set out for young children to curiously investigate. They are an invitation to experience something in their own way and should be thought of as such rather than focussing on adult objectives or ideals.

Process over product: Every time

When working with young children, it is the process, not the product, that is important. Recently, there has been a surge in the popularity of process art as more and more practitioners move away from the worksheet and template mentality. Process art values children and their thinking in a way a template or predetermined outcome never could; it is about 'listening, connecting, empathizing and wondering' (Cherry, 2019: 6) and meeting the child where they are rather than where you expect them to be. This doesn't mean, though, that the outcome of the explorations isn't a fantastic piece of artwork to be celebrated; it just means that the product wasn't the point but rather an added bonus.

It is vital that babies are given the opportunity to explore and follow their fascinations supported by adults who know and trust them. Many early years settings are beginning to move away from handprint–style art beautifully presented to parents and carers, but there is still a lot of work to be done in terms of educating practitioners as to the why and how of engaging creative thinking. It is important that we really understand why we provide the experiences we do and the rationale behind our actions, which are intrinsically linked to our own skills and underpinning knowledge. It is crucial that babies have experienced practitioners working with them who understand the development of babies and all that it encompasses in order to really have an impact in the lives of those youngest children. For managers and leaders in early years settings, it is vital that there is ongoing support for those who may be less experienced or newly qualified, perhaps in the form of leaflets, texts or online courses aimed at babies and children under the age of two.

The early years foundation stage

The current early years framework in the UK, the early years foundation stage (EYFS) consists of guidance that defines the minimum standard for early years settings in order to promote the underpinning principles of the EYFS. The statutory guidance outlines what providers must do under two key sections: welfare requirements and learning and development requirements. This statutory element of the EYFS is supported by a second, nonstatutory set of guidance, known as development matters, that was developed to help and support practitioners as they deliver these outcomes and implement the statutory guidance.

The development matters document outlines the seven areas of learning, which have been separated into two distinct groups: prime and specific areas. These have then been broken down even further into seventeen aspects of learning. Furthermore, throughout the development matters document, each of the four principles have been intricately woven into every area of development, ensuring that practitioners are providing good-quality, meaningful experiences in their day-to-day practice. There is no one-size-fits-all method of using the document, and the development matters is just as it states, guidance. It is down to the professional judgement of those working with it to define their understanding and put it into practice in the best way they can in order to meet the requirements of the EYFS framework and the children that they work with. The characteristics of effective learning also feature in the development matters document as 'interconnected' with the prime and specific areas of learning, and this is designed to acknowledge, respect and build on the various ways in which children learn.

In the EYFS development matters framework used here in the UK, the prime and specific areas of learning are separated, and many practitioners believe there is reason for this. It is commonplace thinking that the prime areas are considered 'more important' and without them, the learning that occurs in the specific areas cannot take place. This is evidenced in many settings around the UK, particularly when it comes to summative assessments and very young children. These usually take place periodically throughout the year in most settings, and up to the age of approximately two years old many settings comment only on the prime areas, potentially discounting development in the other areas of learning. Practitioners are encouraged to use the development matters to support them in delivering high-quality experiences and meaningful interactions with young children, and it is important that the specific areas of development are a part of this for all ages, not just when it is deemed children have achieved enough in the prime areas. As May (2009: 2) describes, 'creativity is one of the basic building blocks of the human species and…is linked to all other areas of learning'. It is therefore important that all areas of learning are taken together, not separated or focussed on to a larger extent, in order to acknowledge the individual nature of the child, their interests and what they are capable of.

Powell and David (cited in Moyles, 2010:247) discuss the contradictory nature of the EYFS and suggest that whilst 'educators are reported to be comfortable…critics suggest that they may be setting playful tasks for the children, rather than allowing them sufficient time and space to exercise their own choice and agency', something which we now know is absolutely vital to the development of creativity.

Invitations to play and explore

Early years is an ever-changing minefield of legislation, both statutory and nonstatutory guidance, and it is because of this I have tried to keep each section as broad as possible, focussing on a range of invitations to play and learning that support all areas. With the early years foundation stage curriculum often in review, I have chosen to define chapters which follow important aspects of development for children and without which other areas such as early numeracy and literacy skills would be unable to be fully explored. However, it needs to be acknowledged that every aspect of the current framework is interlinked and can often overlap in many ways. When going through the invitations, for instance when thinking about water play, it may appear in the chapter 'Discover Physical'; however, we know that simply through talking to your baby, you will have supported their language and communication skills as well as the personal, social and emotional implications of you being present throughout the session. All of the experiences described are in some way linked to developing and supporting creativity in very young children, with many what we would describe as arts based.

The chapters that follow are 'Discover Personal, Social and Emotional', 'Discover Communication and Language', 'Discover Physical' and 'Discover Outdoors'. In each chapter there is a brief introduction to the area of development followed by five sensory experiences, opportunities for learning or invitations to create all suitable for children from birth to two years old. Some of the experiences are age specific, and where adaptions are possible these have been noted, although it is important to use your knowledge of the children you work with and your professional judgement when setting up invitations for young children. All of the recipes that are used are baby safe, which means they are suitable for even very young babies to explore freely (with supervision, of course), but again, you will need to risk assess your own environment and children (particularly those with allergies) in order to ensure they are suitable.

Throughout these invitations to play and create, I have also added where I believe we can support children's repeated patterns of play (schemas), something that is crucial to babies as it gives them the opportunity to practice a range of skills. We have already discussed resources in an earlier chapter, and you will see throughout this part of the book some links to the things we have explored, including recyclable materials, easy-to-use items and budget-friendly options too. Set-up is important because as anyone who has worked with babies knows, babies don't wait. When thinking about offering any type of materials (art based or otherwise), it is important that we create something that looks inviting to babies. We need to tell them we 'care about art-making and value creativity' (Cherry, 2019: 13) and that we want them to do the same. Set-up should be simple yet effective, and the key is to prepare what you will need so that you don't have to worry about painted babies crawling around the carpets or not having everything you need.

The invitations that follow are firm favourites with most children aged zero to two years. Of course there will be exceptions based on temperament, a given mood or the circumstances of the day. Remember, whether you are just starting out on your journey working with babies or are an experienced practitioner, it is important that you are present, focussed and attentive to the needs of the babies you have. If a particular experience isn't going the way you had hoped, that's okay. It is important to lose our preconceived ideas about how an activity will develop and let the baby take the lead. They are curious explorers, and it is guaranteed that they will be gaining valuable skills and sensory input, and their brain will be developing in ways we can only imagine. If you are still a subscriber to the conveyor craft mentality, printing the body parts of babies for parents and focussing on the product of an activity rather than the amazing process and exploration it took to get there, that's okay for now. I accept that it will take time to change what has been the way for some practitioners for many years, but I hope that I have come some way in sharing my experience and knowledge with you throughout this book and that you have seen there is another way, a better way, of igniting our babies' curiosity and, in turn, sparking lifelong creativity.

A note about edible play

Lots of settings have their own rules with regard to edible play and play that uses food as a medium. This is completely dependent on your setting's policy. At my own setting, we believe there is great value in play that involves different kinds of food. The colours, textures and smells that are associated with real food are rarely available with any other medium and cannot be easily replicated. We are careful to supervise babies at all times, use only fresh produce (or pantry staples) and do not believe that it detracts from teaching babies the importance of mealtimes. If food play is not something that you are able to engage with, please skip these or try some of the alternatives. If you do want to try some of the invitations, please ensure you risk assess and take into account allergies and intolerances.

9 Discover personal, social and emotional

A baby's personal, social and emotional development relies heavily on the adults around them. Babies are innately social and seek contact with others from birth. In this chapter, I have provided five opportunities for practitioners to engage with babies to support them in discovering more about themselves, their identities and what their bodies can do. The great thing about this particular area of learning is that in order to be successful, practitioners really only need to be present and attentive and take their cues and responses from the baby. There is very minimal set-up for activities that promote this area of development in particular, as simply spending time with babies, at their level, engaging in nonverbal communication such as eye contact and smiling can have immensely positive effects.

Invitations in this chapter include:

■ mirror play (photo credit: Jo Wise, photographer; Squirrels Family and Childcare Centre)

■ baby bracelets

■ large-scale free painting (photo credit: Wally's Day Nursery)

■ sensory water bowls (photo credit: Wally's Day Nursery)

■ jelly play (photo credit: Laura Brothwell)

Mirror and reflective play

Providing mirrors for babies gives them a unique opportunity to explore their perception of self as well as the reflective properties of mirrors. This is a perfect activity for any age baby, as you can adjust the activity depending on the age of the child. Younger children from birth to nine months may be happy to simply sit, lie or roll onto or near a mirror, watching their reflection. As they get older, you need to challenge and stimulate their brains a little more. From about ten months on, try these ideas:

- Add silver pots and pans for baby to bang on.

- Have a collection of silver resources available in a treasure basket.

- Provide small pots of paint for babies to make marks on mirrors.

- Add shaving foam or gloop to the top of the mirror and ask them to find themselves.

- Provide sponges and a small bucket for the children to wash small mirrors. (Children love small responsibilities, particularly around the age of twenty months when their understanding is beginning to develop even more).

- Take the mirrors outdoors and watch the reflection of the trees or other natural surroundings, commenting and adding vocabulary.

- Use tubes and tunnels outdoors for babies to observe how light changes.

Squirrels Family and Childcare Centre staff provided this invitation for babies to explore mirrors by offering them the opportunity to make marks with water.

Baby bracelets

Younger babies are learning what their bodies can do every minute of the day. If you have young babies in your setting (from around three months), this is a great introductory activity to encourage gross motor movement and the development of skills that require coordination. Loosely tie helium balloons, bells or anything that they can watch or that makes a noise to babies' feet whilst they are lying on their back (if using balloons please supervise and never leave a baby unattended). The added weight will encourage the babies to move their limbs, gaining strength and encouraging them to watch and listen for the sound. Babies are great imitators, so attach a set of what you have chosen to your own arms or legs and lie down next to the baby; talk to them and respond to their vocalisations.

This is a great listening activity for older babies too. They will be able to understand simple instructions and can shake when you shake or stop when you stop. It will also aid naming of body parts as you support children to find a given part.

Supporting schemas

This activity is perfect for babies who have an emerging trajectory or rotation schema.

Large-scale free painting

Paint! Who doesn't love paint? When working with babies, it is important to share the experience with them, no matter how messy it might get. I once watched a practitioner paint with latex gloves on; without even opening her mouth, she had already told the children, 'I don't want to get messy'. We cannot expect children to do anything that we are not prepared to do ourselves, so if you want them to truly embrace paint and enjoy it for everything it has to offer, take the gloves off and watch the curiosity take over.

In this invitation to explore paint in large quantities, babies were offered large basins of paint on a large tarpaulin. They had the opportunity to test their own theories of height, texture and terrain as the climbing frame was covered to protect it. This is a powder paint mix, so please supervise younger babies, but this activity is suitable for all if you are confident that you can manage it. The cleanup is the hardest part, so prepare buckets and baths beforehand and you can be quick to clean babies up when they have finished.

Babies love excess, so this is the perfect opportunity to discover the things they can do with large amounts. We are forever telling young children 'that's enough, I think that's too much now, maybe we should do another colour'. If you look deeper into the actions of the baby and allow them to fully experiment, you will see some crucial learning going on. If babies are never allowed to use to excess, they will never learn to self-regulate.

- Always supervise babies around large amounts of paint.

- They may slip as paint gets onto the floor – this is okay and is again valuable learning, but be close by and on hand to provide reassurance and balance.

- Have paper close by and print the marks babies make to display alongside photographs if possible.

Supporting schemas

There is so much learning in this simple invitation. Babies can be supported in their transporting schema, exploring speed and movement as part of a trajectory schema. Mixing colours of paint or adding other mediums transforms the experience.

Sensory water bowls

Water has a very calming effect on babies; whenever there are babies that are struggling to settle, perhaps in their first few days, my go-to activity is always water play. The feelings surrounding water, its calmness and the senses it stimulates, are relaxing. Using this as a basis, it is a very

versatile, free resource that can be added to in order to create a range of experiences. As I have mentioned, any type of food-based sensory play is so exciting to watch. As young babies explore all their senses, their creative minds go into overdrive as they explore and investigate the colours, smells and textures of what has been offered. Even for those who are unsure, adding this type of experience to water will draw them in and keep them engaged for prolonged periods of time, with very little set-up time needed, (of course, it is always important to ensure it looks inviting to children). Water activities are suitable for babies from the age of approximately six months.

- For younger babies who are not yet sitting, I would suggest smaller containers so that they can get access to the water easily.

- You could always fill a small baby bath so that young babies can fully enjoy the experience (adding warm water is great too).

- Always ensure you stay close to young babies when they are exploring water and stay vigilant. Never leave a baby unattended in water. If you need a towel, nappy or extra resource, ask a colleague to fetch it or watch the children so you can get what you need.

Supporting schemas

Water bowls help to develop all kinds of patterns of play, but by adding different fruits or vegetables, you can support an enveloping schema (by covering them in water and trying to hide them), a transporting schema (by allowing children to move the vegetables from one bowl to another) and a transforming schema (as they poke and prod the vegetables and watch the difference it makes to the water, the texture and the shape).

Jelly play

Playing with jelly provides another medium that is difficult to emulate with anything else. Practitioners can make jelly in a variety of moulds and colours to enhance learning. If babies are interested in a particular book or story, props can be added for babies to 'dig' out, and there is also the possibility to use loose parts, sticks, cones and other materials to poke, squeeze, squelch and squish the jelly.

■ It is a great resource for introducing more vocabulary for older babies.

■ Younger babies can be encouraged to use their whole bodies to explore.

■ Put on some music and see if this changes how the babies interact with the invitation to play.

These photographs courtesy of Laura from Stone Hen Childcare and Squirrels Family and Childcare Centre show how the different provocations can be set up with natural flower petals or loose parts to enhance the invitation.

10 Discover communication and language

It can be argued that communication and language, its acquisition, the understanding of it and our ability to express our thoughts, emotions and ideas effectivity is one of the most important aspects of being human. It is what sets us apart from all other species, and the characteristics of good communication are developed early on in childhood.

We have seen how babies are social from birth. They reach out and connect with their world instantly, from the first cries and eye contact and then to the development of babble and eventually single words. This ability is not something that will develop on its own. Evidence shows us that there is a crucial time (also known as the critical period) when children are able to learn language at an astonishing rate and that after this period has passed, language acquisition becomes much more difficult. As educators, it is our responsibility to ensure that we give children the best possible start to their language journey by encouraging all forms of communication and providing an environment and experiences that support this area of development. Books, props and puppets are all staples in early years settings, but in this chapter, I share some exciting ways these can be used differently to create curiosity amongst our smallest children.

Invitations in this chapter include:

- all about me
- literacy enhancements (photo credit: Stone Hen Childcare, Wally's Day Nursery and Squirrels Family and Childcare Centre)
- sensory small world
- mix and mess using dry and wet ingredients (photo credit: Wally's Day Nursery)
- no-mess sensory bags (photo credit: Wally's Day Nursery)

All about me

The easiest way to support young children's communication and language abilities is to talk to them. We have seen how babies are sociable from birth and thrive on consistent and sensitive interaction from familiar adults.

Ask parents for photographs of the children and their families to display around the baby room. Having these familiar images will often calm babies who are upset. You could also create booklets using the photographs to share with young children and encourage them to talk to you about what and who they can see. Images where the baby is doing something are most helpful as even if you aren't aware of who the person is, you can comment on where they are and what they are doing.

At Wally's we ask the parents of all of our babies to provide what we call a 'chatterbox' when they start with us. This is usually a box (but can be a bag or other container) of familiar objects from home. We keep them for the first six weeks to aid the transition into the setting. As well as providing comfort for settling babies, the objects create a way to engage with babies and allow them to show staff their belongings. This gives children a sense of self and confidence in sharing things that are important to them.

In this activity, practitioners should take the lead from the child and not try to force a certain type of response from the child. Allow them to sit, lie down or kneel at their box and open it on their own. This gives them ownership and shows them that they are important and that we are waiting for them to direct their own intentions.

Supporting schemas

The most obvious pattern of play here is the opportunity to empty and fill their box repeatedly. Practitioners may be tempted to tell a child to 'leave the things out now' or 'stop putting them back in'. This is not helpful to a baby who is learning about the world through this schematic

behaviour. Instead allow them a space to empty and fill as many times as they choose and comment on what they are doing, extending their understanding:

■ 'Oh, I can see your taking all of your things out. Is the box empty now?'

■ 'I wonder what you're going to do next.'

■ Count the objects as they move them or label the items to build on the use of naming and single words, but be careful not to intrude or interfere with the baby's agenda. Sometimes silence is golden.

Literacy baskets and enhancements

It is easy to bring literacy into all aspects of a baby's day. With a few simple enhancements, practitioners are able to support babies' emerging interest in sounds, words and language. The key is to spark their curiosity and provide experiences that will interest them where they are rather than where you would like them to be in their development. It doesn't have to be overly complicated or take lots of time, and more often than not we already have the resources we need. Sometimes it is about thinking outside of the box rather than reverting to a simple storytelling, singing session or just providing crayons. As we can see from the photographs, good-quality literacy enhancements can use a range of materials and mediums and are suitable for a range of ages.

■ Bags, open-top baskets or transparent containers will ensure that babies can see inside (this will spark their imaginations and lead to increased attention).

■ Try setting out a few of the objects alongside a story so that children are offered options in their play.

■ Sit close by so that you can provide comments and 'I wonder' questions to young children. Many practitioners find it difficult to talk to young babies because they don't communicate the way older children do. Take time to sit and observe, and you will find their language speaks volumes even if they are preverbal.

■ For younger babies, focus on sensory experiences, textures and scents. For older babies, you can begin to introduce simple games and other skills that incorporate fine and gross motor movements as well as creative opportunities.

■ Adding mark-making materials or mediums that change their shape means that babies can use their fingers to make marks and eventually grasp at implements and tools.

Sensory small world

Similar to literacy baskets, sensory small-world opportunities are perfect for little fingers and creative minds. They allow for a broad range of play options whilst being open-ended in their nature. Many settings, some of whom are featured in this book, have been working towards or have gained the Curiosity Approach accreditation or are focussing on bringing a sense of Hygge to their provision through the Hygge in Early Years Accreditation. The theories underpinning these ideas are primarily focussed on creating high-quality provision. They focus on a return to natural materials, aesthetically designed environments and a reduction in shop-bought plastic toys. That

said, many of these settings will still retain some of their small-world items. This is because children like small world, and for babies, it is a point of reference. Rubber ducks, dinosaurs, people – these 'plastic' additions can enhance natural set-ups to create something meaningful for young children who may not yet have a point of reference to imagine that a stick is a person.

Lots of practitioners are continuing to set up fantastic small-world play experiences for young children. Here is an example of how dinosaurs and trains can be used whilst still holding on to the calm, tranquil atmosphere.

Adding a sensory element will capture and keep young children's interests – for example, providing different textures, adding water or coloured water beads, wooden discs and leaves and sticks adds to the overall feeling of the importance we place on these types of opportunities. It also means that babies can begin to make connections and use resources in a creative way, using their imaginations and finding and testing their own ideas alongside knowledgeable practitioners.

■ Younger babies will need supervision around small loose parts.

■ Leave your expectations at the door. As we have seen, staff can often set up beautiful play spaces and then become authoritarian in the way that it is played with, hoping to keep it 'nice'. Babies are not interested in how long it took to set up (as these invitations can take as little or as long as you have); they just want to play, and by attempting to direct their play you will inevitably stop the creative processes involved in using their imaginations and the available props for their own agenda.

Supporting schemas

If you have a child with a particular schema, these can almost always be provided for in this type of invitation to play. Adding a potion and mixing option can create an added experience and caters for those who are interested in transforming things.

Mix and mess using dry and wet ingredients

Suitable for babies from three months, this invitation to explore creativity focusses on providing a range of dry ingredients for babies to mix and mess – literally.

At Wally's we love providing this for the children as they use their imaginations to investigate and explore. It should be offered with small pots, dishes and spoons, but sticks can also be added for mixing. In fact, this is the perfect opportunity for in-the-moment planning as you can observe what the children are doing and extend it by adding different tools, materials or water. Children can work on their fine and gross motor movements as well as making marks and filling and emptying their chosen containers. Older babies will enjoy using their imaginations and pulling on their role-play knowledge and imitation of adults by creating and mixing cakes and pies. By offering children baking trays or cupcake cases, practitioners can offer the opportunity to scaffold and extend children's learning.

■ If your resources are edible or taste-safe, then younger babies can explore freely (under supervision).

■ The key to a successful mix-and-mess session is accepting the mess and viewing it as an integral part of the experience. Sharing in the joy of this activity with children in a vital part of its success. If babies see adults walking around after them with a dustpan and brush, it doesn't send the message that we value and embrace their learning.

Supporting schemas

There isn't a schema that exists that isn't encouraged and supported in this activity.

Connection

Children can use added media such as play dough to create structures and can combine the items in their bowl to join things. Adding water creates a sticky dough for children to stick things into too.

Positioning

Children can order or stack their resources in any which way they choose. The great thing about this is that there are no preconceived ideas about how it should go.

Transporting

This really doesn't take any explanation. Let the children move, transport, pick up items and objects and explore their own ideas.

Transforming

Any form of transformation is beautiful to watch during the activity. The key is to provide opportunities for change (adding water or small pots of powder paint), mixing and stirring to make pies and exploring textures by squeezing, squishing and squelching.

Enveloping

By ensuring that you have provided enough of each medium, children will have the chance to develop this pattern of play by hiding loose parts such as stones, pinecones and sticks.

No-mess sensory bags

For those who are not quite ready for super messy activities, these no-mess sensory bags are a great way to explore with babies. They allow babies of any age to investigate the properties of different types of materials as well as texture, temperature and colour, and bags can be created in a range of sizes.

Simply buy some sandwich bags with zipper tops (the clear ones are the best since the print won't detract from the contents) and add a range of stimulating objects and mediums. For this particular activity ours included:

- a snake covered in sand – perfect for an enveloping schema

- chickpeas (amazing for fine motor skills and squishing)

- water and sequins (we used leaves in autumn colours)

- a yellow-themed bag with sweetcorn and rubber ducks (water and lily pad would also support the idea of a pond to accompany a story for a literacy set-up)

- glitter and water

- a squashy frog and baby shampoo – creating bubbles the more the children play

- porridge oats (this could be accompanied by hiding items too)

- marbles and corn syrup (we had some on the shelf from last year and it is not readily available in the UK – hair gel will create the same dense effect as the marbles will slide slowly through the gel)

These are particularly good for children who are also unsure about dirty hands and feet. They can begin their explorations safe and reassured that they will not get mess on them. When they are comfortable, with adult support perhaps, open some of the bags for them to put their hands in and try feeling them.

Discover physical

Physical development is another one of those important areas of learning that often gets overlooked. This is because lots of practitioners believe that physical skills will be acquired whether or not they are encouraged. It is true that there are certain physical milestones that will be learnt regardless of whether we offer babies the opportunity to develop them or not – for example, the ability to sit up or walk. These are not skills that need to be taught as such as they are usually naturally occurring milestones.

For other skills, such as the ability to hold a pencil correctly, use scissors or jump safely, we need to provide a range of exciting, stimulating experiences while children are young that will enable these skills to develop when the time is right and they are developmentally able. The benefits of activities that support fine motor skills are endless, and while we are not thinking about writing sentences just yet, it is true that in order for their bodies to develop the necessary strength and muscles, we need to provide activities designed to support them. The more babies and young children have the opportunity to practice large-scale movements and manipulate materials with their hands, the more successful they will become at knowing what their bodies are capable of.

Invitations in this chapter include:

- dough (photo credit: Wally's Day Nursery)

- baby-safe paint (photo credit: Wally's Day Nursery)

- sand – that's not sand

- mashed potato construction

- shaving foam marks (Wally's Day Nursery)

Baby-safe (sensitive skin) dough

Dough is the perfect resource for busy little fingers, but normal play dough (the kind that contains salt) can often be an irritant for sensitive skin. With more and more children starting nursery with skin conditions and allergies, it is important that they don't miss out on this excellent medium.

For baby-safe dough, you will need:

- 1/2 cup hot water

- 2/3 cup porridge oats

- 3 tablespoons coconut oil

- 1 tablespoon honey

- 2 cups cornflour

I like to use cups where I can because it is the easiest way to measure out ingredients. It doesn't matter what size cup you use as long as it is the same one throughout. Add all the ingredients together (except the cornflour) until the oats start to soften, then add the cornflour and form a dough. Simple. I wouldn't advise adding artificial food colouring, but natural food dyes would be a great addition to your dough. We added herbs to ours and kept a little of the dough back for a bath-rub.

This dough can be set up with herbs, loose parts and sticks for mark making and sensory exploration. It can also be added to bricks to stick them together (for older babies) or even rolled between the toes of smaller babies. Easy to set up and easy to carry out, this is great for babies of all ages and requires little or no adult direction.

Supporting schemas

Definitely one for the transformers, dough lends itself spectacularly to this schema. Shaping and reshaping, adding materials, building upwards and using it for mark making will inevitably change its form into a variety of different shapes and sizes.

Baby-safe paint

I take a lot of my own inspiration from various texts, online resources (I'd defy you to find an early years educator who hasn't heard of Pinterest) and more importantly the children that I work with. Getting to know their interests and fascinations is one of the best ways to make sure you are providing an enriched range of invitations to explore.

Babies love food. Whatever their age, they are learning about the different textures and tastes. Even in utero, babies become accustomed to tastes, and this continues once born. Babies will actively seek their mother's milk or alternative food source from birth, and once weaning begins (around the age of six months) a whole other world opens up in terms of the tastes and sensations that they will experience for the rest of their lives. One of my favourite activities is a sensory paint invitation. Using natural yoghurt (or a lactose-free alternative), simply blend

the required amount with a range of fruits and vegetables to create a sensational opportunity for babies to explore their senses. I like to keep this particular opportunity as natural as possible by using fruits, vegetables and spices rather than adding food colouring, as you can get some amazing colours using only a few spices and natural ingredients without having to enhance them.

This invitation to explore paint, texture and scent really doesn't need any introduction. The joy of working with babies is that they will take what you provide and do magical things with it. I suggest transparent jars or containers for the 'paint', as seeing the colours will entice babies and spark their curiosity.

■ Setting up a neutral sheet of fabric on the floor means that you won't have to worry about the mess and babies can make marks freely.

■ Let babies pick up, smell, taste and use their hands to get to the paint.

- Provide a platter of ingredients that were used to make the paint. Introduce vocabulary to older babies.

- By using fresh fruits and vegetables, younger babies can make connections between their senses.

Supporting schemas

There really is no limit to supporting any type of schema with this play. Babies who enjoy disconnecting can tear and break off pieces of fruit or squash and squeeze them or mix the paint colours to satisfy a transforming pattern or play. Rising twos can line up the paint pots or lots of the same type of fruit or vegetables (for example, piling up spinach leaves or lining up blueberries to introduce language of number and size), and if you make enough paint (as it can get very messy) babies can enjoy submerging their whole hands in the pots.

Sand – that's not sand

There is a lot of debate about whether babies should have access to sand and, if they do, whether it should be accessible at all times. In our setting young babies do not have access to sand, and it is not something that our older babies play with very often, until they are ready to transition into the toddlers where they have a large immersive sandpit. If they did, they may miss out on a whole range of sensory experiences that can mimic sand in a taste-safe way.

■ Weetabix! Empty the contents of a box of Weetabix into a blender and blend until fine.

■ Add some oats, crackers and crispy rice cereal to the food processor and blend until it is a fine sand-like consistency.

For this, quantities don't really matter. The more you use, the more sand you will end up with. It will depend on the size of the container you have to fill and the number of babies you want to engage. Again, this is suitable for children of all ages, but please supervise closely and check for intolerances. It can be treated like normal sand, although with nothing to bind it together, it's not great for sandcastles. You can always add a little bit of water or provide it in a bucket for babies to add independently.

Mashed potato construction

Similar to the sand recipe above, this idea is an alternative to sand for young children. You can make fresh mashed potato, but I find the packets of smash make for a better building consistency. Easy to make, and it's ready in less than five minutes. The only thing to remember is that you will need to wait for it to cool down. It can be soothing to leave it slightly warm for younger babies who can be laid down to play, encouraging movement of their arms and legs and whole bodies. Older babies can use it similarly to how they would use ordinary sand, and as it has a better consistency, it is easily moulded.

■ Natural loose parts and authentic resources can enhance this activity.

■ Babies can begin to build structures and pile it up into a tower.

■ New vocabulary can be introduced as babies play to give meaning to their experiences.

Supporting schemas

Particularly good for children who like to build, join things or knock things down, smash sand can be used to support a positioning schema too. If you have slightly older babies, you can introduce a role-play element into the play using plates and bowls for babies to imitate everyday actions they may have seen at home.

Shaving foam prints

This is an amazing process art activity for babies. Aimed more towards children between the ages of approximately sixteen months and two years, it involves spreading shaving foam and glue in a tray and adding colouring to create a design. There is really no limit to the time that can be spent on this activity, and babies often get carried away. If you provide baking trays covered in shaving foam and small transparent pots for babies to see the bright colours, they can (and probably will) choose to tip all of their colour out at once. This is completely normal and shouldn't be stopped as it revisits what we talked about in terms of children using to excess.

Babies can then use sticks or other tools to make marks, swirl the foam and create to their heart's content. Practitioners should be nearby commenting on what the babies are doing but not interfering or 'taking over their art'. Notice cues that indicate they are ready to finish, at which point you can then make a print (should you wish to have something to remember the session). This is a great example of an activity that results in a fantastic end product, but it must be remembered that is not the point. If you do end up with something great, name it and display it – valuing the child's efforts and sending them the message that they matter.

■ Very young babies who are mouthing should probably stay clear of this activity unless you make our taste-safe version.

■ Taste-safe recipe: combine chickpea juice (drained of the chickpeas) and a sprinkle of cream of tartar using an electric whisk until frothy and foam like.

■ Provide a range of implements for babies to make their marks.

■ Offer an array of colours so babies have the choice of what they want to use, and ensure there is enough for all the children.

12 Discover outdoors

The key to ensuring children make progress in the earliest years of their life is to allow them enough time to explore freely in a range of environments. This is crucial both indoors and outdoors, but what stops practitioners from developing experiences outdoors is usually one of two things: a lack of freedom (from managers and leaders), often due to the stringent safety measures surrounding taking children off the premises, or a lack of motivation to engage children outside in activities that excite them.

In this chapter I have outlined my favourite outdoor experiences that can be done either at your own setting or in the local area. If you are fortunate enough to have a large outdoor space at your setting, you are one of the lucky ones, so pull on your boots and coat and go and explore it. Not only will children enjoy spending time outside developing their physical skills, but they will also be covering many other aspects of learning. If your outdoor space is on the smaller side, this does not mean that you have to forfeit the fantastic opportunities the outdoors brings. Children are very adaptable and will enjoy any space, often using it in innovative ways we might never have thought of. It is true babies need space to explore, but they are only little, and what may appear only a small space to an adult could be a vast area for a young baby.

Invitations in this chapter include:

- wild water play (photo credit: Louise Day)
- soil and plant play (photo credit: Lucy Day/Carlene Cox-Newton)
- sticky nature frames (photo credit: Wally's Day Nursery)
- sensory paths (photo credit: Wally's Day Nursery)

Wild water play

As those of you working with young children know, water is a fantastic, free resource that is very versatile in terms of the things you can do with it, but often practitioners stay within the realms of what they know. Wild water is a natural twist on playing with water from a tap and means playing or engaging with naturally occurring water in the wilderness.

Ideally, wild water play should be done outside, in the wild, at the source of the water, whether it is a waterfall, stream, river or puddle. If you don't have access to these, then playing in the puddles in your outdoor environment or collecting rainwater is a great alternative. Many practitioners and parents shy away from such play, and in doing so babies and children are missing out on vital learning, sensory input and building up a range of other skills, including perseverance and resilience. Playing with wild water boosts babies' immune systems by building up tolerances and supports physical skills including balance and development of proprioception.

Like many of the ideas in this book, wild water comes with its own warning – please do not think I am suggesting taking babies out into freezing cold lakes and streams in the winter in inappropriate clothing. We have a duty of care to ensure our babies are safe, and all opportunities to play should be risk assessed. I am, however, suggesting that with the right support from a knowledgeable adult, appropriate clothing (or barefoot) and increased knowledge surrounding the benefits of earthing, (that is, direct contact with the earth), babies can enjoy all aspects of the natural world safely. As previously mentioned, babies do not get ill from being outdoors; they get unwell due to sedentary lifestyles, inappropriate attire for adventures and contact with others who are unwell.

- All babies can enjoy aspects of wild water play.

- Please ensure you have risk assessed and that you always supervise.

- Wild water is, by nature, usually cold. This doesn't mean that babies can't enjoy short periods exploring it; it simply means practitioners will need to ensure babies are dressed in warm layers and are quickly dried following any session.

- Older babies will enjoy adding things to their water and the sensory experience of textures of logs and sticks.

- If babies are hesitant to fully embrace water, then practitioners can provide small jars for babies to fill with water and experiment creatively but indirectly.

Soil and plant play

Soil- and plant-based activities also tend to be something that adults shy away from with young children, but I truly believe that when the adults supporting children have the knowledge and confidence to support babies in their activities, the children get so much more out of them. We don't all have to become botanists; a simple search of the internet will reveal everything you would need to know about providing safe flora and fauna for babies and young children.

Inside the setting, environments should be filled with the natural world, and shop-bought flowers are usually safe to have around young children. Using flowers and petals is a great multisensory experience for babies (as well as adding a beautiful splash of colour). If you contact your local florist, they are usually happy to provide you with off cuts or fallen petals and flowers they can no longer use. This is a great environmentally friendly way of bringing in flowers to

your provision, but when out and about, we need to be a little more careful, so try and stick to plants, flowers and trees that you recognise. If you don't have access to these naturally occurring colours, artificial ones provide the same effect and can often be used again.

Soil and seeds are a great provocation for slightly older babies (think those confidently walking and able to handle tools). Simply setting them up is usually enough for babies to be interested.

An important note on soil and mud: Be mindful of the children you have and their tendency to mouth or eat materials. We know that children benefit from 'increased microbial exposure from

animals and plants more than the infinitesimally small chance they'll get an infection because of that association' (Krisch, 2018: 1), but we still must keep them safe.

Close supervision will stop any harm coming to babies from excessive ingestion of soil.

- ■ Mud bricks: Add mud to ice cube trays and freeze. This is great for exploring temperatures and giving babies something tangible to hold.

- ■ Mud paint: Adding water and spices to soil can produce some fantastic shades of brown. Team this with sticks for a complete creative art session.

- ■ Planting: Older babies will enjoy scooping and filling flower pots.

- ■ Mud mayhem: Collect mud in a bucket and add water to form a sticky dough. For babies with a trajectory schema, add a vertical white sheet and allow babies to throw and smear mud to their heart's content.

Sticky nature frames

Babies love collecting things, and this is a lovely little invitation to collect natural found resources and objects of interest and get a beautiful child-led outcome to treasure.

Collect cardboard frames or wooden ones that have been donated by families. Take out the glass (if included) and cut out sticky-back plastic to size, pressing the frame down firmly. Replace the discarded piece of the sticky-back plastic over the sticky side (this will preserve the stick). When you are ready to use, remove the back and offer the frames to the children. They can then collect leaves, flowers, sticks and grass and place them on the sticky side.

If you do want to preserve their collection and display their artwork, back at the setting you can press a piece of card or paper to the back (you may need a little glue) and hang.

This is designed for children approximately sixteen months or older, as they will enjoy gathering materials rather than mouthing them.

Supporting schemas

Children who have an interest in connecting things and transporting objects will particularly like this activity. They can collect as many items as they want and carry them with them

on their frame. Younger babies can be given a pot to collect their items that they can then take back to their frame and stick on with adult support if they need it. For those who like to connect and stick things together, the properties of the sticky-back plastic will provide a great spark of curiosity for them to investigate.

Sensory paths

In the final provocation, I wanted to talk some more about sensory paths. These revisit the benefits of barefoot play and the concept of earthing by providing babies the opportunity to experience uneven terrain, different textures and a range of temperatures.

Further to the information I have already provided based on the sensory path we created at my setting, there are lots of ways to provide a similar experience if you haven't got the space to have one permanently. If you are lucky enough to have the space but don't have much budget, why not ask parents to donate. We took inspiration from Pinterest and designed a poster to share with our parents. This made clear what we were trying to achieve, and the donations flooded in. From gravel to pebbles, wooden rounds to plastic tubing, we soon had enough to create our path, and when one of our parents mentioned he was a landscape gardener, he offered his services voluntarily.

Without this, though, the same effect can be created on a budget. Parents can still provide donations of stones, gravel, sand, bark and so on, and these can be offered to children in buckets

or trays. Ideally, they should be as close to the floor as possible as babies can then crawl into them freely. If you have the space, you can always make sectioned areas using logs or bricks to put your sensory materials into (these can also easily be put away).

You can also provide sensory paths indoors. These are simple and quick to make, either by sectioning off squares using logs from outdoors and filling them or by using foam mats with textures placed on them. For a more permanent feature indoors, you could even use a hot glue gun to stick the items down on placemats. These can then be brought out as a set or utilised in other activities such as small-world set-ups or literacy enhancements. Potential materials for indoor sensory paths include:

- feathers

- bath mats or towels

- buttons

- curtain rings

- beads

- sponges

- straws

- plastic bottle tops

- stones

- rope

- pom-poms

- wooden dowels or rounds

Have a go at anything you can find; almost anything makes a sensory, creative, imaginative experience for babies. When creating your own DIY path, please make sure you have used a strong adhesive and do not leave young babies unattended with small parts.

References

Abulof, U. (2017). Why we need Maslow in the twenty-first century. *Society, 54*, 508.

Athey, C. (2006). *Extending thought in young children: A parent-teacher partnership* (2nd ed.). Paul Chapman.

Aynsley-Green, A. (2019). Nurseries 'failing vulnerable children' amid staffing crisis. *The Observer*, September 9, 2019.

Bowlby, J. (1969). *Attachment and loss. Vol. 1 Attachment*. Hogarth Press.

Bronfenbrenner, U. (1995). Developmental psychology through space and time: A future perspective. In P. Moen, G. H. Elder, Jr., & K. Luscher (eds). *Examining lives in context: Perspectives on the ecology of human development*. Washington DC: American Psychological Association.

Bruce, T. (2004). *Cultivating creativity in babies, toddlers and young children*. Hodder & Stoughton.

Bruner, J. (1996). *The culture of education*. Harvard University Press.

Cherry, M. (2019). *Play, make, create: A process art handbook*. Quarto.

Craft, A. (2002). *Creativity and early years education: A lifewide foundation*. Continuum.

Clare, A. (2012). *Creating a learning environment for babies and toddlers*. Sage.

Cohen, D. (2002). *How the child's mind develops*. Routledge.

Compton, A., Johnston, J., Nahmad-Williams, L., & Taylor, K. (2010). *Creative development*. Continuum.

Dahlberg, G., Moss, P. (2005). *Ethics and politics in early childhood education*. Routledge.

Dahlberg, G., Moss, P., & Pence, A. (2007). *Beyond quality in early childhood education & care*. Routledge.

Dahlberg, G., Moss, P., & Pence, A. (2013). *Beyond quality in early childhood education & care*. (3rd ed.). Routledge.

Davies, D., Jindal-Snape, D., Dignby, R., Howe, A., Collier, C., & Hay, P. (July 2014). The roles and development needs of teachers to promote creativity. *Teaching and Teacher Education, 41*, 34–41.

Department for Education. (2013). *92,000 2-year-olds already receiving free childcare* [Press Release] 11th November 2013. Available at https://www.gov.uk/government/news/92000-2-year-olds-already-receiving-free-childcare (Accessed August 2019).

Department for Education. (2017). *Statutory framework for the early years foundation stage*. Available at https://www.gov.uk/government/publications/early-years-foundation-stage-framework--2 (Accessed August 2019).

Donaldson, M. (1992). *Human minds*. Allen Lane.

Drummond, M-J., Lally, M., & Pugh, G. (1989). *Working with children: Developing a curriculum for the early years*. London: NCB/NES.

Duffy, B. (2006). *Supporting creativity and imagination in the early years*. Open University Press.

Duffy, B. (2010). Art in the early years. In J. Moyles (ed). *The Excellence of Play*. Open University Press.

Early Education. (2012). *Development matters in the early years foundation stage*. Department for Education.

Ebrahim, H. (2011). Children as agents in early childhood education. *Education as Change, 15*, 121–131.

Edwards, C. (2002). Three approaches from Europe: Waldorf, Montessori and Reggio Emilia. *Early Childhood Research & Practice, 4*, 1–17.

Egan, K. (1983). *Education and psychology: Plato, Piaget and scientific psychology*. Teachers' College Press.

Einarsottir, J. & Wagner, J. (2006). *Nordic childhoods and early education: Philosophy, research, policy and practice in Denmark, Finland, Iceland, Norway and Sweden.* Information Age Publishing.

Else, P. (2012). *The value of play.* Continuum.

Field, F. (2010). *The foundation years: Preventing poor children becoming poor adults.* Cabinet Office.

Fleer, M. (2010). *Early learning and development: Cultural-historical concepts in play.* Cambridge University Press.

Fumoto, H., Robson, S., Greenfield, S., & Hargreaves, D. (2012). *Young children's creative thinking.* Sage.

Gerhardt, S. (2010). *The selfish society.* Simon & Schuster.

Goldstein, L. (1998). More than gentle smiles and warm hugs: Applying the ethic of care to early childhood education. *Journal of Research in Childhood Education, 12*(2), 244–261.

Goouch, K. (2010). Permission to play. In J. Moyles (ed). *The excellence of play.* Open University Press.

Goouch, K., & Powell, S. (2013). *The baby room: Principles, policy & practice.* Open University Press.

Gottlieb, A. (2000). Where have all the babies gone? Towards an anthropology of infants. *Anthropological Quarterly, 73*(3), 121–132.

Gunning, C. (2016, October 27). Settling children, crying children. https://www.early-education.org.uk/news/new-blog-settling-children-crying-children (Accessed September 2019)

Hanscom, A. (2016). *Balanced and barefoot: How unrestricted outdoor play makes for strong, confident and capable children.* New Harbinger.

Haughey, S. (2020). *Wonder art workshop.* Quarto.

Hellyn, L., & Bennet, S. (2017). *The A to Z of the curiosity approach.* The Curiosity Approach.

Hobson, T. (2019, January 24). Using just the right amount. Available at http://teachertomsblog.blogspot.com/search/label/art?updated-max=2019-05-01T06:18:00-07:00&max-results=20&start=25&by-date=false Accessed September 2019.

James, A., & Prout, A. (1997). *Constructing and reconstructing childhood.* Routledge Falmer.

James, A., Jenks, C., & Prout, A. (1998). *Theorizing childhood.* Polity.

Jarman, E. (2013). *The communication friendly spaces approach.* Elizabeth Jarman Group.

Keenan, T., & Evans, S. (2009). *An introduction to child development* (2nd ed.). Sage.

Kjørholt, A. (2013). Childhood as social investment, rights and the valuing of education. *Children & Society, 27*(4), 245–257.

Knight, S. (2013). *Forest school and outdoor learning in the early years.* Sage.

Kress, G. (1997). *Before writing: Rethinking the paths to literacy.* Routledge.

Krisch, J. (2018, June 11). Parents should let kids eat dirt. It's good for the biome. Health and Science. *https://www.fatherly.com/health-science/let-kids-eat-dirt-gut-health/* (Accessed June 2019)

Lansbury, J. (2012, April 9). Sitting babies up – the downside. Babies' and Newborns' Motor Development. https://www.janetlansbury.com/2012/04/sitting-babies-up-the-downside/ (Accessed August 2019)

Lee, N. (2001). *Childhood and society.* Buckingham: Open University Press.

Lindemann-Matthies, P. & Knecht, S. (2011). Swiss elementary school teachers attitudes toward forest education. *The Journal of Environmental Education, 42*(3), 152–167.

Lindqvist, G. (2003). Vygotsky's theory of creativity. *Creativity Research Journal, 15*(2), 245–251.

Lynch, K. (2007). Love labour as a distinct and non-commodifiable form of care labour. *Sociological Review, 55*(3), 551–570.

Malaguzzi, L. (1993). cited in O'Connor, D. (2012). Creativity in childhood: The role of education. 8th Global Conference: Creative Engagements Thinking with Children. The University of Notre Dame Australia.

Malaguzzi, L. (1993). For an education based on relationships. *Young Children, 49*(1), 9–12.

Manning-Morton, J., & Thorp, M. (2003). *Key times for play.* Open University Press.

Manning-Morton, J., & Thorp, M. (2015). *Two year olds in early years settings: Journeys of discovery.* Open University Press.

Mashford-Scott, A., & Church, A. (2011). Promoting children's agency in early childhood education. *NOVITAS Research on Youth & Language, 5*(1), 15–38.

Maslow, A. H. (1943). A theory of human motivation. *Psychological Review, 50*, 370–396.

May, P. (2009). *Creative Development in the Early Years Foundation Stage.* Routledge.

Mayall, B. (2002). *Towards a Sociology for Childhood, Thinking from Children's Lives.* Open University Press.

Maynard, T., & Waters, J. (2014). *Exploring Outdoor Play in the Early Years.* Open University Press.

McKinney, K. (2012). Adventure into the woods: Pathways to forest schools. *Ontario Journal of Outdoor Education, 24*(3), 24–27.

Millar, S. (1968). *The psychology of play*. Penguin.

Mohammed, R. (2018). *Creative learning in the early years: Nurturing the characteristics of creativity*. Routledge.

Moyles, J. (2010). *The excellence of play*. Open University Press.

National Advisory Committee on Creative and Cultural Education (1999). *All our futures: Creativity, culture and education*. London: DFEE.

Nutbrown, C. (1996). *Respectful educators – Capable learners: Children's rights and early education*. SAGE.

O'Connor, D. (2012). Creativity in childhood: The role of education. 8th Global Conference: Creative Engagements Thinking with Children. The University of Notre Dame Australia.

Page, J. (2011). Do mothers want professional carers to love their babies? *Journal of Early Childhood Research, 9*(3), 310–323.

Pascal, C., & Bertram, T. (2009). Listening to young citizens: The struggle to make real a participatory paradigm in research with young children. *European Early Childhood Education Research Journal, 17*, 249–262.

Pascal, C., & Bertram, T. (2017). Creativity and Critical Thinking are Central to an effective Early Years Curriculum and Pedagogy. BECERA. Available at www.becera.org.uk.

Peleg, N. (2013). Reconceptualising the child's right to development: Children and the capability approach. International Journal of Children's Rights. *21*(3), 523–542.

Pikler, E. (1979). The Competence of an Infant. The Pikler Collection. https://thepiklercollection.weebly.com/uploads/9/4/5/3/9453622/the_competence_of_and_infant_full_-_pikler.pdf

Pikler, E. (1979). *Se Mouvier en Liberte des le Premier Age*. Paris: Presses Univ. de France.

Central Advisory Council for Education (1967). *The Plowden Report, Children & Their Primary Schools*. London: HMSO.

Pound, L. (2005). *How children learn*. Step Forward.

Pound, L. (2011). *Influencing early childhood education*. Open University Press.

Powell, S., & David, T. (2010). Play in the early years. In J. Moyles (ed). *The excellence of play*. Open University Press.

Pugh, G., & Duffy, B. (2013). *Contemporary issues in the early years*. SAGE.

Pungello, E. P., & Kurtz-Costes, B. (1999). Why and how working women choose childcare: A review with a focus on infancy. *Developmental Review, 19*, 31–96.

Qvortrup, J. (1985). Placing Children in the division of labour. In P. Close & R. Collins (eds). *Family and economy in modern society*. London: Macmillan.

Recchia, S., & Dvorakova, K. (2012). How three young toddlers transition from an infant to a toddler child care classroom: Exploring the influence of peer relationships, teacher expectations, and changing social contexts. *Early Education and Development, 23*(2), 181–201.

Rinaldi, C. (1993). The emergent curriculum and social constructivism. In C. Edwards, L. Gandini, & G. Forman (eds). *The hundred languages of children*. Ablex.

Rinaldi, C. (2007). Preface. In G. Dalhberg, P. Moss, & A. Pence (eds) *Beyond quality in early childhood care and education*. Routledge.

Rose, J., & Rogers, S. (2012). *The role of the adult in early years settings*. Open University Press.

Sharp, C. (2004). Developing young children's creativity: What can we learn from research? *Readership Primary*, (32).

Sharpe, M. E. (2004). Imagination and creativity in childhood. *Journal of Russian and East European Psychology, 42*(1), 7–97.

Slade, M., Lowery, C., & Bland K. (2013). Evaluating the impact of forest schools: A collaboration between a university and a primary school. *British Journal of Learning Support, 28*(2), 66–72.

Sommer, D. (2012). *A childhood psychology*. Palgrave Macmillan.

Steiner Waldorf Education. (2009). *Guide to the early years foundation stage in Steiner Waldorf early childhood settings*. Association of Steiner Waldorf Schools.

Stoppard, M. (2005). *Baby's first skills: Help your baby learn through creative play*. Dorling Kindersley.

Striker, S. (2001). *Young at art*. Holt Paperbacks, Henry Holt and Company.

United Nations (1989). *Convention on the rights of the child*. Geneva: United Nations.

Winnicot, D. (1971). *Playing and reality*. Penguin.

Woodhead, M. (2006). Changing perspectives on early childhood: Theory, research and policy. *International Journal of Equity and Innovation in Early Childhood, 4*(2), 1–43.

Vecchi, V. (2010). *Art and creativity in Reggio Emilia: Exploring the role and potential of ateliers in early childhood education*. Routledge.

Vygotsky, L. S. (1978). *Mind in society*. Harvard University Press.

Contributions

- ▪ Wally's Day Nursery
  - Photo credit
    - Jessica Beveridge – Red Rabbit Photography
    - Louise Day
- ▪ Laura Brothwell – Stone Hen Childcare
  - Photo credit – Laura Brothwell
- ▪ Elizabeth Jarman – Managing Director: The Elizabeth Jarman Group
- ▪ Ashley Corcoran – Love of Learning Childcare
  - Photo credit – Ashley Corcoran
- ▪ Martin Pace, Director – Reflections Nursery and Small School
  - Photo credit – Staff at Reflections Nursery, Worthing
  - Photo credit Reflections1 – Jo Wise, photographer
- ▪ Carlene Cox-Newton – Carlene's Cubbyhouse Family Day Care
  - Photo credit – Carlene Cox-Newton
- ▪ Amanda Redwood, Charlotte Blackburn, and Katie Davies – Nina's Nursery High Lane
  - Photo credit – Nina's Nursery High Lane
- ▪ Your Nursery Ltd
  - Photo credit – Your Nursery Ltd
- ▪ CurioCity Childcare
  - Photo credit – CurioCity Childcare
- ▪ Bright Stars Nursery
  - Photo credit – Bright Stars Nursery
- ▪ Shiny Stars Day Nursery
- ▪ Shiny Stars Day Nursery Trentham – Alishia Woodward and Bianca Johnson
  - Photo credit – Shiny Stars Day Nursery
- ▪ Veronica Green E.C.E., B.P.E. – Ronnie's Pre-School
  - Photo credit – Veronica Green
- ▪ Squirrels Family and Childcare Centre, Northampton – the staff tribe and Squirrels' families
  - Photo credit – Squirrels Family and Childcare Centre

Index